The Farmer's Guide to Grain Marketing

Sean K. Treasure

DEDICATION

This book is dedicated to the U.S. farmer whose success I am committed to improving. May he long feed the world, one bushel at a time.

Table of Contents

ACKNOWLEDGMENTS

I would like to thank all the individuals whose insight and constructive critiques went into the development and refinement of the content of this book. I had no idea what I was getting into, but thanks to a great deal of help and encouragement, I am quite proud of the end product. Special thanks to my brothers, Eric and Ryan Treasure for their editing and critique and to my wife Mia for her unwavering support. I am most grateful to be involved in the Agricultural industry in some small way. Special thanks to the all of the producers that I had the opportunity to learn from. You made this possible.

1 GRAIN MARKETING RISKS

When I was in college, I had the opportunity to spend a summer working for the USDA assisting a soil scientist in his studies on wind erosion. Basically, the job involved a lot of grunt work as the cheap labor involved in getting experiments set up. I assisted in the transportation and set up of an enormous "wind tunnel" that was erected on various test plots at the Washington State University research farm in Lind, WA. I also spent countless hours crushing dry soil samples with a 50 pound rolling pin for onsite testing at the university. It was tedious work.

One of the major catalysts for these studies was the tragic accidents that occurred in eastern Oregon on September 25, 1999. In the midst of an especially hot, dry summer, a farmer set about the work of tilling his fields. Winds began kicking up and the dust flew. The resulting dust cloud created black out conditions across I-84 and caused numerous collisions. At least 50 vehicles were involved in accidents going in both directions of the highway. (AP) After the shock of the tragedy wore off, researchers began evaluating the causes. Eventually, focus shifted to farming practices that many thought were at least partially to blame, and funding was allocated with the goal of finding possible solutions to the perceived problem.

Ultimately, the research focused on drawing a contrast between traditional agronomic practices consisting of a winter wheat-summer fallow rotation (which involved at least a few passes over each acre with tilling implements) versus a no-till practice. It was at this point that the wind tunnel came in. We would haul it out from Pullman to Lind every day during the summer and set it up on various plots, some of which were prepared using conventional methods and others were prepared using a no-till method. The researchers measured wind erosion from each of these plots in the form of PM10. That is, particulate matter 10 micrometers in diameter.

It will come as no surprise that the no till plots emitted significantly less PM10 than those plots prepared using conventional methods. No-till farming resulted in substantially less wind erosion and topsoil loss than conventional practices. The benefits in this regard were indisputable. Of course, the economic feasibility for producers in addition to a number of other questions still needed to be answered before the practice could actually be put into commercial use, but that is another story.

The researchers spent untold hours developing and testing the experiment. They put immense amounts of work into creating the wind tunnel to carry out the experiments. There was no framework in place for what they did. A wind tunnel? That was pure imagination. I'm certain that there were plenty of times that they second guessed themselves and perhaps even the methods that they had developed. Then, once they had assembled a large enough data set, which consisted of a number of years of experimentation, they had to analyze and assimilate the information and publish it in a peer reviewed journal. I'm sure it was a daunting task from the start.

Grain marketing is an endeavor that takes real thought, preparation, planning, confidence and perhaps a little imagination. There are so many different moving parts that it can feel overwhelming and at times, completely bewildering. It's easy to second guess a sale, particularly when the market rallies as soon as you've signed the contract. I've had farmers tell me over and over how much they regretted specific sales. Even though most producers understand that this is an incorrect way of thinking, many still exclaim to themselves, "If only I had waited one more week!"

On December 24, 2013, Reuters released an article with the headline "High cash rents to squeeze U.S. Midwest grain farmers in 2014". The gist of the article was simple: landlords wanted more money for their land after five years of record farm income, while at the same time grain prices were trending lower. According to the article, farmers in Northern Illinois had enjoyed average profits of $251 per acre in 2011 and $188 per acre in 2012. The forecast for 2014 was dire: projected losses of $81 per acre. (Stebbins)

Higher input costs coupled with lower revenues would indeed put the squeeze on any business. It seems that farmers face a disproportionate amount of risk year over year relative to other businesses. Farming always has been and will continue to be an uncertain way of life. Anybody who has been in the business for long knows that times of affluence are always followed by times of struggle. Like the biblical story of Joseph who foresaw seven years of plenty followed by seven years of famine and planned accordingly, the most successful farmers are those who manage to not merely survive but actually expand their businesses by seeing these trends and capitalizing on them. They plan for the worst and take calculated risks, always thinking first and foremost about turning a profit, not hitting a home run on every trade.

Kay and Edwards identify five general types of risk farmers' face. These include, production, marketing, financial, legal and personal. (Kay) The grain marketer can successfully manage the marketing (price risk) and production risk. This book focuses on these two types of risk.

The first is price risk, which can be mitigated (but not eliminated) with a sound marketing plan. As a trader, a frequently mentioned adage I heard over the years was "the cure for high prices is high prices." Though oversimplified, there is no question that this is the general nature of grain markets. When prices get "too high" farmers grow more grain, quantity demanded drops and prices necessarily fall, in search of a new equilibrium. Producers who design and stick to a marketing plan put themselves in a better position to manage long term price swings.

Unfortunately, over the last ten years, price volatility has reached levels that have shocked even the most seasoned veterans of the trade. In the past a movement of 2 or 3 cents was considered significant. Today, soybean futures movements of 40 or 50 cents in a day are common place. A single day move of 20 cents in corn is not generally considered a surprise. So, it is completely reasonable to suggest that the price risk that producers face today is more significant than what has been faced in the past. Go in unprepared and un-hedged, and you effectively bet your farm.

The second type of risk we'll address in this book is production risk. What will your yields be next year? What about quality? Nobody can answer these questions accurately, particularly if you're a dry land operator.

The 2010 winter wheat crop in Montana had great expectations only weeks before harvest. In general, yields were in fact quite good. Unfortunately, rain hit the crop hard right before harvest causing a major drop in some milling characteristics, most notably the Falling Number. Falling Number tests measure gluten strength in dough, a factor that flour mills aren't willing to compromise. Both U.S. and overseas buyers insist on minimum Falling Number standards for the wheat they buy. How do you manage this type of risk?

Crop insurance can help mitigate these types of production risks. The dilemma producers face is how to combine grain marketing plans with sufficient crop insurance to maximize returns. What is an appropriate amount to forward contract for next year's crop? Unfortunately, due to an uncertainty of what the correct course of action is, many producers fail to take timely action. This can be costly.

Of course, farmers face all kinds of other risks that won't be addressed here. But, if you can manage the price and yield risk, you will set yourself up to weather the other uncertainties that exist in your line of work.

This book is an outline on how to mitigate these risks in order to make your business as profitable as possible. Yes, farming takes some faith; sowing a seed into bone dry soil and hoping that Mother Nature takes care of it is a pretty unique business to be in. However, that doesn't mean you can't think like a CEO. You're in this business to make money. After you read this book, you should feel comfortable in assembling your own marketing plan and thinking in terms of profits rather than simply wishing for higher prices.

It's time to put an end to the sell and repent mindset that is so prevalent amongst farmers today. Wouldn't it be nice to feel good when you sell grain and not feel as though you've just made a mistake? That is the goal of this book. It will assist you in developing a marketing plan that will reduce risk while maximizing returns. When you put a plan in place and know in advance what it takes for you to run a profitable enterprise, you can market with confidence.

2 THE BIG PICTURE

Ansel Adams was a photographer who began developing his craft in the 1920s. He became famous for his sensational landscapes of the American Southwest. His photographs are still widely reproduced, regarded as some of the most beautiful images of a region known for its stunning array of color. The red rock, blue sky and green cactus were all brought together masterfully, in vivid artistry. Yet, for much of his career, Adams worked only in black and white. How was he able to capture the beauty of the region using a medium that was seemingly so deficient in grasping the varied hues?

Adams brilliantly utilized light and perspective in his work. By simply adjusting the aperture of his camera he was able to control the amount of light allowed to reach the film. He could control how much of the landscape would come into focus, the sharpness, contrast and the brightness of the image. With his skillful touch, perspective of the image was changed. We could see nuances in the landscape that we otherwise would have been unable to see.

You're probably asking yourself, what does this have to do with grain marketing? Well, the grain trade is a large and diverse industry. There are so many facets that it's easy to become focused only on our own small area of responsibility. Thus, a change in perspective is necessary to see the big picture.

From time to time, savvy grain marketers will adjust their apertures in order to ascertain how all of the varied pieces of the trade fit together. Trust me; merchants working at the biggest trading houses in the world are desperate to know exactly what you as a farmer are thinking. Vast resources are spent analyzing you, attempting to outguess you. If that's true, don't you think it's worth a bit of time analyzing what *they're* doing? With that in mind, let's step back and take a macro look at the global grain trade.

International Markets

A major concept economists use to help explain tendencies in international trade is the idea of specialization. Certain countries tend to do specific things very well. Japan makes cars, Saudi Arabia produces oil, and England is a major hub for money and banking. The same is true for agricultural products. Some countries grow certain crops very well, and others have to go out and purchase them in the global market. Thus, some countries are net exporters of grain and others are net importers.

In the United States we grow corn and soybeans exceptionally well. We are also a major wheat producing nation, but it could be argued that our competitive advantage in wheat production isn't as great as it is for corn and soybeans. As a result of our agricultural production prowess, the U.S. is a net exporter of agricultural products (one of the few industries where we have such a surplus). In fact, when all of the goods that comprise the sum total of all US imports are subtracted from the total of all US exports, we can see that the value of imported goods is much greater than the value of our exports. This is known as a trade deficit. The US has been running at a total deficit for some time despite the agricultural surplus.

In the global grain trade we are in constant competition with other exporters for an opportunity to supply those countries that don't produce enough to meet their domestic needs. These countries are the net importers.

Table 1-2014 Top Exporters and Importers of selected products

Major Wheat Exporting Regions	Major Wheat Importing Regions
1. European Union	1. North Africa
2. United States	2. Middle East
3. Russia	3. Southeast Asia
4. Canada	4. Brazil

Major Corn Exporting Regions	Major Corn Importing Regions
1. United States	1. Japan
2. Brazil	2. Mexico
3. Argentina	3. European Union
4. Ukraine	4. South Korea

Major Soybean Exporting Regions	Major Soybean Importing Regions
1. Brazil	1. China
2. United States	2. European Union
3. Argentina	3. Mexico
4. Paraguay	4. Japan

Source: (USDA)

When a buyer decides to purchase grain and oilseeds in the international market, they will often make an official **tender** announcement soliciting offers from potential suppliers. The tender announcement will define the exact quantity, type, quality and shipment period of the desired product as well as the date and time offers are due. Exporters will then submit offer prices based on their individual willingness to sell. At this point, buyers can simply choose the cheapest offer price and enter into a contract with that supplier. Of course, they also always give themselves the option to pass on all offers and re-tender at a later date.

The tender process is extremely competitive not only between exporting countries but also between individual suppliers within each country. In the PNW export market where I worked, as of this writing seven different exporters vying for various sales opportunities. In general, only the most competitive offer price will win a tender. When tenders are scarce, the business of bulk grain exports is a very low margin enterprise. On the other hand, it can be very profitable when export capacity becomes strained due to large export volume. In this sense, export terminals are really in the business of selling elevation capacity as opposed to grain.

There are a large number of companies involved in the global grain trade but it is dominated by a relatively small number of multinational agribusinesses. Louis Dreyfus, Cenex Harvest States, Bunge, Archer Daniels Midland, and Cargill are a few of the commonly known grain majors. But there are others that are if not just as big, are at least equally significant to the international grain trade. The Japanese trading houses of Mitsui, Marubeni and Toyota, the Australian giant Graincorp and Switzerland based Glencore are also actively involved in the global grain trade.

Domestic Markets

Once grain is hauled via truck to a local grain elevator, it can literally end up anywhere in the world. Country terminals have many options depending on their relative location. In addition to shipping grain into the export market, there are a variety of domestic users involved in the process. Flour millers, feedlots, ethanol producers, sweetener plants, oilseed processors, feed mills and biodiesel plants are all contending for the same bushels.

Because of the large number of players in the marketplace, there tends to be inefficiencies. Any one grain merchant can only talk to a relatively small segment of the trade.

Drawing on my own experience once again, as an export merchant, the bulk of my time and energy was spent focused on the PNW market, primarily to feed my own export terminal. I was only casually involved in other marketing opportunities. Consequently, I'm certain that there were times when I sold grain through my company's export terminal when I could have obtained a higher price by shipping it elsewhere. This inefficiency creates opportunities for other players to flourish, including brokers and trading companies. Their goal is generally to profit from these inefficiencies by identifying arbitrage opportunities. We'll address arbitrage later, for now let's focus on the players.

Cash grain brokers are in the business of facilitating trade between commercial traders. They maintain a book of contacts, including both shippers and receivers, and are constantly seeking out bids and offers in an effort to find tradable prices. When brokers are involved, generally the selling party will pay a fee of between ½ cent and 1 cent per bushel on whole grains. For byproducts, good brokers can frequently charge significantly more.

Trading companies provide liquidity to the marketplace in a different way. F In general, a trading company doesn't necessarily have any physical assets in terms of grain infrastructure. The lack of elevators and storage space, though limiting, doesn't prevent a trader from taking positions in the market. A trading company will buy or sell cash grain based on their individual bias on price direction or, if they find the opportunity, they may "back to back" a trade. That is, they will lock in a purchase and a sale simultaneously.

The difference between a trading company and a broker is a matter of physical ownership of the product. Brokers typically don't take any positions, nor do they ever really own the product. Their function is simply to bring buyer and seller together in exchange for a small fee. Trading companies on the other hand, act as a **principle** participant in the exchange. That is to say, they are a responsible party on the contracting documents. They physically buy and sell the products even if they don't actually load or unload them in their own terminals.

There are still others involved in the overall grain and oilseed supply chain. Shipping companies including railroads, barge lines, and trucking operators all have a part to play in the process. On some railroads, the finite quantity of rail freight available in the market is traded just like any other commodity. This market is dominated by a few large players, with the critical mass to manage a large freight deck. Once a railroad sells railcar availability, freight traders in these markets will buy and sell this freight access with country elevators.

This system is generally a relatively efficient process of allocating a scarce resource, but it's not without its struggles. In the 2013/2014 marketing year, rail freight became extremely expensive due to a variety of constraints on rail capacity that essentially resulted in a shortage of railcars. BNSF rail freight reached prices as high as $7,000/car just for the right to load, not including the cost to move the car from origin to destination. Truly, the market was strained.

The Commercial Grain Trade

The world of commercial grain trading is, like farm marketing, one of risk management. Traders take calculated gambles in order to drive profits for themselves. Large companies will leverage positions in one region in an effort to make money in another. This method of profiting between market discrepancies is known as arbitrage and it is a common way for large traders to make money in the market.

Commercial grain traders often refer to themselves as "basis traders." They generally have much smaller flat price positions than they do for basis positions. In other words, their flat price exposure is generally hedged in the futures markets and most of their profits are made on basis positions. A basis position is simply a long or short position with an un-priced futures component. A flat price position includes futures and basis.

When commercial traders buy and sell amongst each other they will trade basis only and price futures by exchanging futures positions. In this way, it is not necessary for them to take a futures position at all (though most do anyway).

These **paper market**s involve substantial quantities of grain and are basically a way for commercial grain companies to manage their cash positions. When one wants to be long, another will want to be short at a given market price and delivery point. Typically, they are bought and sold basis major delivery points such as the Gulf Export market or the Hereford feed market. This way, it is relatively easy to trade in and out of a position in the same market area. Additionally, there is generally a common set of terms and grade specifications to further simplify the process and avoid confusion. This trade provides liquidity to the market place in the commercial grain world but it also impacts basis levels.

Commercial grain trading houses are notoriously secretive and competitive. They treasure information and use it to their advantage. If one of them is aware of information that hasn't hit the market yet, perhaps a piece of export business that was sold, he may attempt to buy cash grain from other commercials before prices go up. Many old timers will remember the "Great Grain Robbery" of the 1970's. Russia bought thousands of metric tons in secret, once the market found out, prices skyrocketed. Though there are now safeguards in place to prevent that from happening again (the USDA now requires immediate reporting of overnight sales of 100,000 MT or more), the point remains the same. Large commercial basis traders can have a significant impact on cash grain prices.

<u>Arbitrage</u>

Earlier, I mentioned that inefficiencies exist in the marketplace that afford firms such as brokers and trading companies an opportunity to participate in the commercial grain trade. These inefficiencies often result in price discrepancies between one region and another or between related assets (similar wheat classes for example).

For example, there was a time in my career when we were buying high protein HRW from Texas and shipping it to export terminals in the PNW. This is not something that happens very often; in fact, many of the old timers had never seen this type of movement. The high protein HRW was undervalued in Texas relative to what it was worth in the PNW. So, the arbitrage opportunity was to benefit from the price discrepancy created by relatively cheap Texas values and relatively expensive PNW values.

But, that wasn't the end of it. The market took the arbitrage a step further. The high protein Texas HRW was used as a blend into the more valuable Dark Northern Spring Wheat. In essence, the Texas HRW was nothing more than inexpensive DNS. Through the miracle of arbitrage, HRW was magically turned into DNS. As an aside, when making these types of blends, grain handlers must be aware of the grade specifications they are selling. There are generally tolerances for "wheat of other classes" (WOCL). As long as they keep the blend within contract tolerances it is a perfectly acceptable practice.

A successful merchant will work to identify these price discrepancies and profit from them. By simultaneously buying in the undervalued region and selling in the overvalued region, he can effectively benefit from the spread.

Let's say that corn is trading at a basis of 50 over delivered Chicago and 100 over delivered Hereford. All else being equal, it would make more sense to ship to Hereford, right? In theory, more corn would ship to Hereford, driving the price down there. Similarly, less would be sold into the Chicago market. The reduced supply would result in higher prices there. The prices would converge until there was parity between the markets.

Figure 1-Relative Basis

Chicago (Basis =+50)

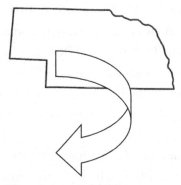

Hereford (Basis =+100)

Of course, this example is grossly oversimplified. Merchants must manage freight spreads and be in constant engagement with a variety of market areas in order to quickly identify these arbitrage opportunities before they're gone. For example, if it costs 50 cents per bushel to ship corn from Country Elevator A to Chicago and 1.50 per bushel to ship to Hereford, Chicago is actually the more profitable alternative for Elevator A's corn. Throw in another elevator that's closer to Hereford and the opposite might be true.

Figure 2-Relative Basis Including Freight Costs

Chicago (Basis =+50, Freight =-50)

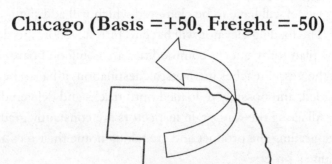

Hereford (Basis =+100, Freight =-150)

The takeaway here is that the market is always evolving. Arbitrage opportunities exist all the time, but typically only for a short time before more traders jump on the bandwagon and restore parity to the asset.

Ocean Freight and Exchange Rates

To price-sensitive flour millers in Indonesia all that really matters is the net cost of wheat in local currency delivered to their mill. Obviously this net price is the sum of a number of cost factors including a number of freight conveyances.

Consider for a moment all of the costs that are added to grain once it leaves your bin. First and foremost, the cost for you to truck it to your local elevator which includes not only fuel and wear and tear on your truck, but may also incorporate additional charges for hired hands to do the work (or the value of your own labor). The elevator will then take a margin on that grain. They may then need to truck it to another facility to accumulate enough to load on a train or barge. Barge and rail freight cost money just for the right to load it, in addition to the actual freight rate to get it wherever it's going. There may even be additional costs in the form of **demurrage** if the companies involved can't unload the train or barge in a timely manner. From there, the exporting company will take their cut of the profits. An ocean-going vessel will have to be chartered which will add significant cost. The loading elevator will have to hire stevedores to develop a stow plan for whatever commodities are going on board. Then, once the vessel reaches its overseas destination, it has to be offloaded, and possibly re-loaded onto trucks and delivered to the mill. All along the way, grain inspectors are constantly grading and re-grading the product and are taking home their fees as well. It's quite a process.

Figure 3- Supply Chain Flowchart

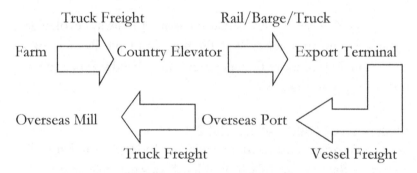

So, the end result is, the price that flour mill in Indonesia pays is much different from the price you are seeing at the local elevator. Frankly, foreign buyers are not really concerned with the price of a bushel of corn in Iowa. All they care about is the cost on a landed basis at their facility. More importantly, they care about the price spread between U.S. corn and Brazilian corn on a landed basis. Aside from the domestic price of grain, the biggest factors affecting this price are vessel freight and currency exchange rates.

Vessel freight, sometimes referred to as ocean freight is a dynamic, ever-changing market. It trades much like any other commodity with bids and asks defining the value of the product. The big trading houses like Louis Dreyfus, as well as a number of companies specializing in vessel freight, negotiate not only with vessel owners but also with each other to establish a market price.

The Baltic Dry Index (BDI) is a figure that reflects the price of moving bulk cargoes by sea. It is issued on a daily basis by the London-based Baltic Exchange. This number is established by a consortium of international ship-brokers who collectively determine their estimate of the current freight market. Supply and demand factors influence the market price of vessel freight in the same way as anything else. In 2008, the BDI reached record high levels as buyers clamored for grain. Anybody who was farming in 2008 will remember that year as long as they live but it was a big one for everybody involved in the trade. Within six months however, the BDI had dropped 94%. When the dust settled, many shipping companies were barely scraping by.

In addition to evaluating the cost of freight as published by the BDI, the USDA publishes a report every Thursday that delves into the many transportation issues of the grain industry. The Grain Transportation Report (GTR) not only includes information on rail and barge prices and movements, but also container statistics, volume numbers by port and ocean freight trends. If you're attempting to evaluate U.S. competitiveness in the world, one of the most important factors to pay attention to are the freight price spreads. On the following page is a table taken directly from the September 25, 2014 GTR.

Table 2- GTR Sample Freight Rates

Ocean Freight Rates for Selected Shipments, Week Ending 09/20/2014

Export Region	Import Region	Grain Types	Loading Date	Volume loads (metric tons)	Freight rate (US$/metric tons)
U.S. Gulf	China	Heavy Grain	Oct 10/20	60,000	45.00
U.S. Gulf	China	Heavy Grain	Oct 1/10	57,000	45.50
U.S. Gulf	China	Heavy Grain	Oct 1/10	60,000	45.50
U.S. Gulf	China	Heavy Grain	Sep 20/Oct 10	55,000	45.25
U.S. Gulf	Djibouti	Sorghum	Sep 10/24	24,000	106.41
U.S. Gulf	Mexico	Heavy Grain	Aug 2/6	33,000	11.25
PNW	China	Heavy Grain	Nov 1/30	60,000	26.50
PNW	Philippines	Grain	Aug 1/15	65,000	22.50
Brazil	China	Heavy Grain	Sep 1/10	60,000	34.00
Brazil	China	Grain	Aug 20/30	60,000	31.50
Brazil	China	Grain	Aug 10/31	60,000	33.25
Brazil	China	Grain	Aug 1/30	65,000	35.50
Germany	Iran	Wheat	Aug 20/Sep 8	65,000	35.00
River Plate	China	Heavy Grain	Aug 1/31	60,000	44.50
River Plate	Philippines	Soybean meal	Sep 20/27	40,000	40.00

Rates shown are for metric ton (2,204.6 lbs. = 1 metric ton), F.O.B., except where otherwise indicates; op=option

What can you glean from this report? First of all, just looking at the snapshot provided we can see that it's cheaper to ship grain to China from Brazil than it is out of the US. But there's something more important to consider: it's not the cost on any given day that you should be concerned with. At a $15 spread, China might still buy US grain if the landed price is competitive. What you need to evaluate is the *trend* in the overall spread. The GTR will also provide this information including comparison's of today's values versus a year ago.

The other major factor for overseas buyers is exchange rates. They are perhaps the more frequently mentioned component in the press. It's not uncommon for agricultural journalists to cite moving a strengthening dollar as the reason for softening futures prices. In international trade, as a local currency gains value relative to other currencies, the local currency has more buying power. Conversely, they have less export power as their goods are now relatively more expensive to importing nations. Once deals are done and payment is received, traders must convert from dollars to their own local currency.

↑ Value of US $ relative to other currency ⟶ ↓ US Exports

In general, international trade is conducted in U.S. dollars, as the world's "reserve currency." International traders in the United States have a somewhat easier time conducting business since they typically won't have to convert to any other type of currency. Foreign exchange risk thus lies with our buyers. The important thing for us to consider is once again price spreads. In other words, the value of our buyers' currency in dollar terms, relative to the value of our buyers' currency in our competitors' currency terms. Sounds complicated and frankly, it is somewhat. At the end of the day, the value of the US dollar is inversely related to export volumes of all US goods.

Putting it all together

Ok, clearly there is more information out there than anybody can possibly digest in a meaningful way. The point is to keep you engaged in the market. In my trading days, I sometimes dabbled in a specific market that wasn't part of my bread and butter business. For example, though 95% of my business was related to the PNW export market, I also traded the cash HRW market in Kansas City. I never made a lot of money there but by being involved in that market, I was more educated on the market for HRW as a whole and I believe it helped me achieve better results in the PNW. For you, that means staying on top of other markets that you're not necessarily actively involved in so that you can have a better feel for trends in your business.

The grain trade is a large and diverse industry with many business subsets stemming from it. Each piece represents a critical component to the overall movement of grain from the farm to end users around the world. Having read this chapter you should have a somewhat better view of the big picture of the grain market. Though each participant may have an important role to play, it is important to remember that they are all for-profit institutions. Everyone is in the business to make money; the important takeaway for producers is to market wisely. There are no freebies for any of us. And, there isn't anybody watching out for your business but you.

3 PLANNING FOR PROFITABILITY

<u>Pre-Planting Planning</u>

Before the seed drill ever hits dirt, you will have made a number of decisions that ultimately impact your success as a farmer. You're the CEO of your operation and as the CEO you are tasked with the responsibility of making money year in and year out. To do that, you have to plan in advance what your money-making strategy will be. That strategy may be different next year than it was last year; it's up to you to re-evaluate the market and implement varied strategies in order to grow your business. The first step in that is to figure out what you're going to grow.

Estimating Production Costs

For most growers, there are at least a few different options in terms of what crop to put in the ground. For example, you're probably not limited to growing just one class of wheat. Perhaps you can produce cotton, corn or soybeans. Maybe peas, lentils, or potatoes are an option. In order to determine the crops that will generate the most profit for your enterprise, you must first estimate production costs for each crop.

Fortunately, the process is a relatively simple one. In a nutshell, it involves summarizing income and expenses for each crop. You'll begin by breaking your expenses into fixed and variable categories. **Fixed costs** refer to those expenses that arise simply from being in business regardless of what crop you plant or even whether you plant a crop or not. For example, you will pay property taxes even if you don't use your land. As you construct cost estimates for various crops, your fixed expenses will remain unchanged. In other words, they will be the same regardless of the crops you decide to plant.

Variable costs are those expenses that arise from the operation of your business. For example, drying costs for a corn crop won't be incurred unless you grow a corn crop. Similarly, fertilizer costs will be different for wheat than they are for soybeans and will be non-existent if you don't plant anything. Furthermore, variable costs will generally increase as your planted acres increase.

Figure 1- Production Costs Budget

Fixed Costs	
Land	$
Property Taxes	$
Equipment	$
Depreciation	$
Miscellaneous	$
Variable Costs	

Fertilizer	$
Seed	$
Chemicals	$
Application	$
Custom Harvesting	$
Drying	$
Assessments	$
Labor	$
Interest	$
Fuel/lubrication	$
Repairs	$
Irrigation	$
Miscellaneous	$
Total Expenses	$

Fixed Costs

Land: For producers who are renting property this is a relatively easy figure to calculate. If you have a cash lease, add the total cost per acre into your fixed costs. A crop share lease is a bit more complicated as you'll have to estimate yield and price. I find the simplest way to do this is to assume average yields for the particular field and the current market price for harvest delivery of grain.

If you own the land you are farming, don't make the mistake of not accounting for land costs. Many producers fail to account for the value of their land. How much could you rent it out for if you weren't farming it yourself? You may have to come up with some composites by asking your neighbors what they're paying for rent. Once you find out, plug this number into your fixed costs. The key is to not sell you short. After all, you may be able to make a decent living just renting your land out.

Property Taxes: Tax on all land and buildings. If you're leasing 100% of your operation you may not have any property tax expense.

Equipment: This will include interest on equipment loans as well as any taxes and insurance. In some states, machinery is subject to property tax. You may decide to break out interest expenses from other equipment costs which is completely appropriate if you want to further dissect the nuts and bolts of your finances.

Depreciation: Depreciation expense on all farm assets should be included here. Since there are several ways assets can be depreciated out over their useful life, you may need to talk with your accountant to find out whether this cost will remain flat from year to year or whether it will change. Though this is particularly important for tax purposes, it's also an expense that impacts your net P&L so it needs to be included here.

Variable Costs
Seed, Fertilizer, Chemicals: Determine how much you'll need for each different crop so you can make the comparison.
Remember, you'll need to calculate on a per acre basis.

Application: Cost per acre of custom application. Again, there will be variability from one type of crop to another so calculate for each.

Custom Harvesting: This expense brings up the same concept that we encountered in valuing land. For producers who don't hire custom harvesters, the concept of opportunity cost has to come into play. If you were to sell your services to your neighbor instead of cutting your own crop, what could you get for it? The opportunity cost of harvesting your own crop is the lost income of selling your services to your neighbor. In my opinion, this figure should be plugged in regardless of whether you hire outside help or not.

Grain Drying: If you own your own drying equipment, you'll need to estimate the cost of fuel to operate it. Depreciation on this equipment will be included as a fixed cost above. If you pay your local elevator to dry your grain, simply find out the per bushel cost from them. You'll have to assume average yields and plug in the cost per acre.

Assessments: This includes any "check off" dollars used to fund various grain commissions.

Labor: This is easy if you have hired hands working on your farm. Additionally, don't forget to include the value of your own labor on your farm. Again, the concept of opportunity cost comes into play. You could take a job in town rather than work on the farm. What are you worth?

Interest: As a variable expense, this includes only interest on money that is tied up in operating expenses. For example, if you borrowed against your credit line in order to pay input costs, the interest accrued would be entered here. This will not include interest on capital expenditures such as machinery and land which is included as a fixed expense above. Calculate the variable interest expense for each crop option.

Fuel/Lubrication: This may be tough to estimate but a strong effort must be made to project these costs. A good place to start is to look at your fuel consumption in prior years and then adjust that usage for current fuel prices. Once a total has been estimated, calculate on a per acre basis.

Repairs: There's no accurate way to forecast when you'll have an equipment breakdown. So, a good rule of thumb is to budget 2% of the purchase price of new equipment for repairs. Older equipment may require a modified figure, projecting higher repair costs.

Irrigation: Cost per acre for water rights. This is critical for irrigated farms as some crops take a lot more water to produce than others. Depending on your allotment, the crops requiring more water may be much more profitable for you. The only way to know for sure is to run the numbers.

Pre planting P&L Analysis

Each crop that you estimated production costs for in step 1 will result in a different return and all have varying risks associated with them. Again, the goal is to plant the crops with the greatest return within appropriate rotational considerations.

The first thing you'll need to do is create a table to determine net profit on a per acre basis that looks something like this:

	Production Cost	Yield	Price	Net Profit
HRW	230	40	$7.00	$50.00
Sorghum	250	45	$8.00	$110.00
Corn	450	160	$4.00	$190.00
Soybeans	300	40	$12.00	$180.00

Obviously, you'll have to make some assumptions regarding your production costs, yield and price. We've already addressed assumptions for estimating production costs. For estimating yields, I recommend actually running the analysis using three separate yield estimates. The first will be an average estimate using either historical numbers from your farm or, if you haven't grown the crop before making an educated guess on average yields. If you are considering planting a crop that you haven't grown before, it might be worth taking the time to visit with your local extension agent to come up with a more educated guess.

The second and third will be best and worst case scenarios. Be sure and include farming practices that impact yields such as crop rotation when you're making yield assumptions. By plugging the array of possible yields for HRW into our first table, we come up with the following:

Production Cost

HRW	230	**40**	$7.00	$50.00
	230	**10**	$7.00	-$160.00
	230	**80**	$7.00	$330.00

The array of possibilities ranges from very a profitable $330/acre to a disastrous loss of $160/acre. Of course, the price could move substantially but for budgeting purposes, the only accurate estimate is to use the current market. We'll address appropriate hedging and risk management methods in a later chapter. For now, the takeaway is to come up with an approximate "average" return. We'll use the best and worst case scenarios as we assemble the marketing plan.

As mentioned, the price could change down the road but your estimate on price will simply be the market price available to you should you forward contract your crop right now. Notice that the forecasted price in the HRW matrix doesn't change based on the forecasted yield in either the best or worst case scenarios. The market price is the market price. It's that simple. You don't need to over think this piece by attempting to forecast price movements. In fact, it would be imprudent to do so and likely a good way to compromise the accuracy of your profit estimates. Make it easy on yourself and simply find where you could forward contract your crop TODAY.

The shipment period you select to determine your forward contract price is up to you. My rules for grain marketing say that if the market pays you to carry (and you can financially manage deferring payment) then sell a deferred date instead of the "gut slot" of harvest. Shipment periods could differ from one commodity to the next in your analysis and that is completely acceptable. Remember, this number is simply a realistic price that you can expect to get for your crop.

If we put it all together using the above example we come up with the following:

	Production Cost	Yield	Price	Net Profit
HRW	**230**	**40**	**$7.00**	**$50.00**
	230	10	$7.00	-$160.00
	230	80	$7.00	$330.00
Sorghum	**250**	**40**	**$8.00**	**$70.00**
	250	10	$8.00	-$170.00
	250	80	$8.00	$390.00
Corn	**450**	**160**	**$4.00**	**$190.00**
	450	50	$4.00	-$250.00
	450	240	$4.00	$510.00
Soybeans	**300**	**40**	**$12.00**	**$180.00**
	300	10	$12.00	-$180.00
	300	65	$12.00	$480.00

Based on our figures in the matrix, assuming normal yields for our ground, corn is the most profitable crop to grow, beating out soybeans by $10.00/acre. The best case yield scenario is informational only at this time and the worst case scenario will be used later on when considering crop insurance needs. Obviously, you'll have rotational considerations for your specific operation but the analysis tells us to lean toward planting additional corn acres.

Using the matrix you've created you should have a pretty good idea of where the most profit potential lies. Congratulations, you know what crops you'll be planting this year and have a good idea of what your cash flow will look like under different yield scenarios.

Break Even Analysis

Once you've created realistic forecasts for input costs and production, you'll need to estimate your breakeven cost. This is an important step for grain marketers as it allows you to make informed business decisions. My number one rule for grain marketing is to focus on business profits. Knowing what it takes to turn a profit is critical to any successful enterprise, particularly for farms.

Half the work is already done since you've already assembled estimates for production costs and an array of yields. Calculating break even prices is simple. Simply divide the production cost per acre by your estimated yield per acre.

Cost per acre/ yield per acre = Break Even Price per bushel

Using the corn example, it would look like this:

$450/160 = $2.8125

So, assuming your yields averaged 160 bushels per acre, you'd need to sell your corn for at least $2.8125/bushel in order to break even. Any price below that and you're operating at a loss; any price above that and you're operating at a gain. 160 bushels per acre isn't the only possibility though. Let's run a best and worst case scenario to see what the other possibilities are.

	Production Cost	Yield	Break Even Price
Corn	**450**	**160**	**$2.8125**
	450	50	$9.00
	450	240	$1.875

Under the worst case scenario, we'd need to market our corn for $9.00/bushel just to break even. That's a daunting thought under most circumstances. This figure is important though as it will guide you in evaluating your crop insurance needs.

Post Harvest Adjustments

Once your grain is cut and binned, it's likely that some of your estimates will need to be adjusted to accommodate actual yield. If you skip this step, your breakeven calculation could be off significantly from where it actually should be. Clearly this could have a big impact on your ability to market profitably. To make the adjustments, simply plug your actual yield for each crop into the breakeven price calculation. It may also be necessary to adjust actual per acre production costs if they are different from your budgeted estimates.

Cash Flow Budgeting

With just a cursory read through my grain marketing rules and you'll see that I'm not crazy about letting cash flow needs dictate marketing decisions. The reason for this is simply because this may force you into making poor sales. Still, it can't completely be ignored. Nobody can hold grain indefinitely if market carries last for years. At some point you have to pull the trigger. Establishing a cash flow budget will help you see precisely where you need money to pay bills. This way, you can see cash flow picture many months in advance and look for the best marketing opportunities to keep your operation moving forward.

William Edwards of Iowa State University Extension and Outreach created a 12 step method of developing a cash flow budget:

1) Outline your tentative plans for livestock and crop production. You've already developed some tentative plans for crop planting after going through the first half of this chapter.
2) Take an inventory of livestock on hand and crops in storage now. If a recent financial statement is available, information found under the current assets section can be used.

3) Estimate feed requirements for the proposed livestock program.
4) Estimate feed available including supplies on hand and expected new crop production.
5) Estimate livestock sales.
6) Estimate sales of non-feed crops.
7) Estimate income from other sources.
8) Project crop expenses and other farm operating expenditures.
9) Consider any capital purchases you may make this year.
10) Summarize debt payments.
11) Estimate non-farm expenditures including family living expenses.
12) Sum total cash inflows and total cash outflows. (Edwards)

Once you have assembled the necessary information, you can organize it on a month by month basis. I recommend a 1 year cash flow budget that is updated regularly so you can plan forward contracts. In reality, the timing of your cash flow needs probably won't vary much from one year to the next but going through the exercise of updating the information will force you to re-evaluate your needs and plan accordingly.

Treasure Farm		2015 Cash Flow Budget		
	Total:	January	February	March
Beginning cash balance:	$10,000	$6,500	$35,000	-$31,500
Operating Cash Inflow				
Sales of Crops	$250,000	$0	$0	$250,000
Livestock	$305,000	$250,000	$35,000	$20,000
USDA Payments	$0	$0	$0	$0
Farm rents/Custom Hire	$0	$0	$0	$0
Other	$3,000	$1,000	$1,000	$1,000
Capital Cash Inflow				
Breeding Livestock	$12,000	$0	$12,000	$0
Machinery and Equipment	$0	$0	$0	$0
Nonfarm Income				
Wages/Salary	$7,500	$2,500	$2,500	$2,500
Investments	$3,000	$1,000	$1,000	$1,000
Total Cash Inflow	**$590,500**	**$261,000**	**$86,500**	**$243,000**

Operating Cash Outflow				
Seed	$60,000	$40,000	$10,000	$10,000
Fertilizer	$125,000	$75,000	$20,000	$30,000
Chemicals	$40,000	$0	$0	$40,000
Other Crop Expenses	$60,000	$20,000	$15,000	$25,000
Gas, oil, lube	$45,000	$15,000	$15,000	$15,000
Hired Labor	$6,000	$2,000	$2,000	$2,000
Machine Hire	$9,000	$3,000	$3,000	$3,000
Feed	$60,000	$20,000	$20,000	$20,000
Feeder Livestock	$30,000	$10,000	$10,000	$10,000
Veterinarian	$4,500	$1,500	$1,500	$1,500
Machinery Repairs	$8,500	$2,500	$5,000	$1,000
Building Repairs	$5,000	$5,000	$0	$0
Cash Rent	$50,000		$0	$50,000
Supplies	$3,000	$1,000	$1,000	$1,000
Property Taxes	$5,000	$5,000	$0	$0
Insurance	$12,000	$10,000	$1,000	$1,000
Utilities	$1,500	$500	$500	$500
Auto	$3,000	$1,000	$1,000	$1,000
Loan Payments	$24,000	$8,000	$8,000	$8,000
Family Living Expenses	$12,000	$4,000	$4,000	$4,000
Other	$13,500	$2,500	$1,000	$10,000
Total Cash Outflow	**$577,000**	**$226,000**	**$118,000**	**$233,000**

In this example, you'll see a net cash outflow for February and March. There are 4 possible solutions to manage the problem. First, you can use surpluses in prior months to cover the shortfall. In other words, your business funds the shortfall via existing cash on hand. Second, you can borrow money to cover the shortfall and pay it back when net cash inflows exceed outflows. Third, you can attempt to decrease your cash outflows for March. Or fourth, you can increase your cash inflows for March by selling more products.

Any of these solutions can work; the key is to find the most profitable alternative. If your rate of interest on borrowed funds is very low it might make the most sense to simply draw on your credit line. If the market is giving you sell signals, the most profitable alternative may be to sell more grain.

Proper planning is critical to developing your overall grain marketing plan. Without it, you are effectively flying blind, throwing darts and betting the farm. The time spent on careful budgeting will make you money in the end. Remember, the second rule of grain marketing is to know your costs of production.

4 THE ROLE OF CROP INSURANCE

If insurance in the form of put and call options is part of a comprehensive grain marketing plan (see chapter 7), then crop insurance is a no brainer. It happens each and every year: a late hailstorm wipes out the wheat crop just prior to harvest. A late freeze results in winterkill, destroying the corn. When disaster strikes as it inevitably will, you'll be grateful that your operation is protected. Additionally, crops that are adequately insured give you increased flexibility in making marketing decisions which allows you to forward contract grain more confidently. Therefore, crop insurance allows insured parties to take advantage of marketing opportunities quicker and with greater ease than their un-insured neighbors.

Insurance that covers specific disasters such as crop-hail insurance has been available for some time. These types of policies are intuitive; the tangible loss in production is relatively easy for insurers to measure. As time went by, other products developed. Multi-peril crop insurance based on actual production history (MPCI-APH) broadened protection to cover yield losses from many causes, in addition to the traditional hail coverage. More recently, policies have been introduced to insure gross revenue rather than yield.

The 2014 farm bill instituted a number of changes to the federal crop insurance program. Not only has the alphabet soup that you've become accustomed to changed, there are also many material changes to the program that you need to be aware of. Gone are GRP and GRIP. They have been replaced by AYP and ARP. Though the basic premise of the policies remains the same, the nuts and bolts have changed. Producers must understand the product that they are enrolling in; it's not just a one year deal. You're locked into your selected program for a period of five years. I recommend going over the details with your crop insurance advisor. Additionally, many land grant universities offer seminars that help one to understand the minutiae of the crop insurance offerings in the current farm bill.

Because the details of crop insurance change with each farm bill they are beyond the scope of this book. So, I'll cover the basics and discuss how crop insurance fits into a comprehensive marketing strategy.

First of all, it's important to have an understanding of some of the basic terminology in order to make an informed decision. The most fundamental component and the first decision you'll have to make is what type of insurance units to use. When enrolling in the crop insurance program, farmers have the ability to decide how to split their insurable acreage into separate units according to four different methods.

Insurance Units

The base element of a crop insurance policy is the insurance unit. A unit is defined as each piece of land that is insured independently of other pieces. So, a single farming operation can have more than one insurance unit, though it is not required. Consequently, it is possible to experience an insurable loss on one unit and not on others. As a general practice, many producers prefer to divide their farms into as many units as possible in order to diversify their protection across separate, smaller areas. As we'll see, though this may not be a bad strategy, it comes at a price.

Basic Units

A basic unit is defined as all of one crop in a county for all of your owned or cash rented acres. Furthermore, each share rent landowner arrangement would be a separate basic unit. So, if you are growing corn on land that you own as well as on land that you have rented via a crop share contract, you would have at least two basic units. If you are renting additional land via a crop share contract with another landowner, that would qualify as a third basic unit. Crop share landowners can also insure their interest in the crop as a separate unit.

If however, you are renting additional land via a cash lease agreement, that crop would be lumped into your owned land. So, a cash rented field and your owned land would be only one basic unit, not two separate units.

Different crops will create separate units. Say for example you are growing corn in one field and soybeans in another. That would be at least two separate units. If, you are growing corn in two different counties that also qualifies as separate units and must be insured separately. As was mentioned earlier, since we're dealing with separate insurable units it's possible to receive an indemnity payment on one crop and not on another. This seems like an incentive to divide your production into as many units as possible but keep in mind that will mean a lot more record keeping. Separate production records must be kept for each basic unit so there is more work involved.

Optional Units

An optional unit is similar to a basic unit except it is further divided into township sections. A producer can also designate an optional unit for a crop that is grown under distinctly different production practices. For example, if one field is irrigated and another is dry-land, you may be able to divide them into separate optional units and insure them separately. Bear in mind, it doesn't matter if it's divided into township sections or by varying production methods, you'll need to keep separate production records for each optional unit.

Enterprise Units

An enterprise unit is a simplified way to manage your crop insurance needs. Essentially, it combines all acres of a single crop within a county into a single unit, regardless of whether they are owned or rented, or how many landlords are involved. So, instead of having separate units for each share crop lease and each piece of owned or cash leased land within a county, you could elect to have only one unit for each crop. There are a few qualifications however. First, there must be at least two basic units to combine to form an enterprise unit. Second, the crop must be grown in at least two township sections within a county, and at least two of the sections must have the smaller of 20 acres or 20 percent of the total area of that crop.

The benefit of the enterprise unit is simplicity. There isn't as much record keeping and you don't have as many insurance policies to maintain. Clearly, a large operation growing multiple crops across several counties could become a headache if you elect basic or optional units. However, because you are spreading risk across your entire operation, overall yields will tend to be less variable than when focusing on smaller units so your odds of receiving an indemnity payment are lower for enterprise units. Subsequently, premiums will also be lower.

Whole Farm Unit

Last of all is the whole farm unit. It further simplifies the responsibilities of the grower and the insurer. The whole farm unit combines multiple crops into a single policy. As a result, whole farm units are available only for revenue protection policies due to the variations in yields between one crop and another. Again, the benefit is simplicity and discounted premiums. The amount of the discount will depend on the proportion of the total acres planted to each crop. Additionally, the premium subsidy is also higher for whole farm units at higher levels of coverage.

The following table and accompanying explanation comes from the University of Iowa Extension and Outreach. It illustrates possible division of units for a number of farms owned by a single operator.

Figure 1- Insurance Units

Farm A owned	Farm B 50 - 50 crop share lease from Smith	Farm D cash rent lease from Jones	Township Section 2
Township Section 1	Farm C cash rent lease from Smith	Farm E 50 - 50 crop share lease from Smith	
Farm F owned		Farm G 60 - 40 crop share lease from Black	
Township Section 12		Township Section 11	

Basic units

This operation would qualify for three basic units.
Unit 1 includes Farms A, C, D, and F (all owned or cash rented).
Unit 2 includes Farms B and E (both crop share rented from Smith).
Unit 3 includes Farm G (crop share rented from Black).

Optional units

This operation would qualify for six optional units.
Unit 1 includes Farms A and C (owned or cash rented in Section 1).

Unit 2 includes Farm B (crop share rented in Section 1).
Unit 3 includes Farm D (cash rented in Section 2).
Unit 4 includes Farm E (crop share rented in Section 2).
Unit 5 includes Farm F (owned in Section 12).
Unit 6 includes Farm G (crop share rented in Section 11).

Enterprise units
This operation would qualify for one enterprise unit, including all the farms shown. If more than one crop was being grown, or if some farms were located in a different county, additional enterprise units could be designated.

Whole farm unit
If both corn and soybeans were being grown on the farms shown, all acres could be combined into a single whole farm unit. Additional whole farm units could be designated in other counties. (Plastina and Edwards, Proven Yields and Insurance Units for Crop Insurance)

Multi Peril Crop Insurance (MPCI)

Multi peril crop insurance provides comprehensive coverage against weather related losses as well as a number of other perils. It is subsidized by the Federal government in varying levels depending on the type and amount of coverage you purchase. You have various options in electing coverage, we'll discuss those next.

Yield Based Protection

Yield Protection insures producers against yield losses due to some natural causes and offers a production guarantee based on individual **APH (Actual Production History)**. Producers can select coverage levels between 55% and 85% in increments of 5%. You can also select the percent of the projected price you want to insure between 55 and 100 per cent. The projected price is determined in accordance with the **Commodity Exchange Price Provisions** and is based on daily settlement prices for specified futures contracts. For example, the projected prices for corn and soybeans are, respectively, the averages of December and November CBOT futures contract prices during February. (USDA-RMA)

For yield based protection, the gross indemnity is calculated as the bushels per acre loss (production guarantee minus actual yields) times the projected price. So, if the harvested plus any appraised production is less than the yield insured the farmer is paid an indemnity based on the difference. Indemnities are calculated by multiplying this difference by the insured percentage of the projected price selected when crop insurance was purchased and by the insured share.

Example:

Let's say you are planning to grow 1,000 acres of soybeans. Your proven APH yield is 40 bushels per acre. Since yield protection is available in any 5% production increment from 55% to 85% of your proven yield, you could choose any of the following coverage levels:

Table 1- Sample coverage levels for YP insurance

Coverage Level	Yield Guarantee (bpa)
55%	22
60%	24
65%	26
70%	28
75%	30
80%	32
85%	34

Let's say that you elect the 75% coverage level. Let's also say that you choose to insure at the highest possible price guarantee of $10.50/bushel. If a drought cuts your yield to 25 bushels per acre, you would receive an indemnity payment on the loss:

$$(30 - 25)*\$10.50 = \$52.50 \text{ per acre}$$

You would receive a total indemnity payment of $52,500 on your 1,000 acres of covered soybeans.

Obviously, the higher the level of coverage you elect to purchase, the higher the premium will be. Once again the question you must ask yourself is how much loss can I afford? Is a 22 bushel per acre yield sufficient to cover your expenses and allow you to continue operation? If so, the minimum coverage might be right for you. It is likely that some higher level will be necessary however.

Revenue Protection

Just like yield based protection, revenue protection insures producers against some natural causes but it also covers revenue losses caused by a change in the harvest price from the projected price. Again, you will select the amount of coverage you would like in 5% increments from 50 to 85 per cent of APH. The **projected price** and the harvest price are 100 per cent of the amounts determined in accordance with the Commodity Exchange Price Provisions. The amount of insurance protection is based on the greater of the projected price or the harvest price. The Harvest Prices for corn and soybeans are, respectively, the average of December and November CBOT futures contract prices during October. If the harvest price is less than the amount of insurance protection, indemnities are calculated by subtracting the harvest price from the value insured and multiplied by the amount of coverage.

Example:

Using the same figures as we used for the yield protection example, let's say you instead elect to purchase revenue protection, again based on a proven yield of 40 bushels per acre. Assuming the insurance price is $12.35 per bushel you could elect any of the following coverages:

Table 2- Sample coverage levels for RP insurance

Coverage Level	Price Guarantee
55%	$6.79
60%	$7.41
65%	$8.03
70%	$8.65
75%	$9.26
80%	$9.88
85%	$10.50

Let's say you elect 85% coverage and your yield comes in at 32 bushels per acre. You will receive an indemnity payment if your net revenue is less than $420/acre (40*$10.50= $420/acre). So, if the price of soybeans has risen sufficiently, you may not receive any payment. However, you are guaranteed minimum revenue of $420/acre. Anything less will generate an indemnity payment. Still, you retain the right to gain if prices appreciate significantly. As a result, this policy carries a higher premium than the Revenue Protection with Harvest Price Exclusion policy which will be covered next.

Revenue Protection with Harvest Price Exclusion

This plan is similar to revenue protection but carries a lower premium. The reason for this is that the revenue guarantee is determined by the projected price only. In other words, producers give up the opportunity to benefit from higher harvest prices. Indemnities are paid if the amount harvested plus any appraised production multiplied by harvest price is less than the amount of insurance protection.

Catastrophic Coverage

Catastrophic coverage (CAT) compensates farmers for crop yield losses exceeding 50% of their APH at a payment rate of 55% of the projected price. In order to receive an indemnity payment under CAT coverage, producers must realize a yield loss of more than 50%. The indemnity payment is only on losses exceeding the 50% threshold. Producers pay no premium for CAT coverage. A $300 per crop, per county administrative fee is required except in cases of financial hardship.

Area Yield Protection (AYP)

AYP protection is similar to standard yield protection with one major difference. Where typical yield protection uses 'unit' yields as the basis for indemnity payments, AYP protection uses county yields. Interestingly, this coverage was developed with the assumption that if any single producer's yields are significantly lower, the rest of a given county will also be lower. The difference in indemnities can be significant either for better or worse since yields should be somewhat less variable when an entire county's production is taken into consideration. Because of this lower variability, premiums are also generally lower for area protection.

When weighing the benefits of one policy versus another, you'll need to know yield expectations. This figure is determined using historical National Agricultural Statistics Service county average yields and adjusted by the Federal Crop Insurance Corporation. The USDA RMS publishes this information on an annual basis.

The net indemnity payment considers two variables that aren't included in the YP calculation. These are the **protection factor** and the **loss limit factor.**

The protection factor adjusts the amount of coverage, similar to the coverage level. Producers choose any protection factor from 0.8 to 1.2. Higher protection factors will result in correspondingly higher indemnity payments and higher premiums for coverage. Lower protection factors result in lower indemnities and premium payments.

The loss limit factor represents the percentage of the expected county yield at which no additional indemnity amount is payable, and it is currently set at 0.18 (Plastina, Current Crop Insurance Policies). In other words, the bottom 18% of the expected county yield won't receive indemnity payments.

So, the bottom line for AYP is that whether or not you receive an indemnity payment depends entirely on how the county as a whole produces. If you have record yields but the rest of the county suffers inexplicable yield losses, you will still likely receive an indemnity payment. Similarly, if you're yields are a fraction of what you expected but the rest of the county out produces expectations, you probably won't receive a payment. Though these are unlikely scenarios you should still consider your ability to sustain losses before enrolling.

Area Revenue Protection (ARP)

Much like the standard RP policy, the ARP protects against revenue losses resulting from county level production losses, low prices or a combination of both. It also allows for upside price protection which could result in higher indemnities if the harvest price is higher than the projected price. Essentially, this policy establishes a minimum price for producers. Like AYP, ARP uses county level revenue as opposed to unit revenue.

Producers will once again need to choose a coverage level and a protection factor (from .8 to 1.2). Indemnities are dependent on county yields and projected prices. Like RP, prices are established by CEPP and approved by the RMA.

Area Revenue Protection with Harvest Price Exclusion (ARPHPE)

Like ARP, ARPHPE allows producers to receive an indemnity payment when there is a county level production loss, low prices or some combination of the two. In fact, this policy is virtually the same as ARP except that it does not allow for upside price protection. So, rather than having the option of using the harvest price in your indemnity calculation, the 'projected price' established prior to seeding will be used. Subsequently, policy premiums will be lower for this type as opposed to ARP.

Area Catastrophic Coverage (ACAT)

This policy is exactly the same as the unit level CAT coverage policy except that once again, indemnities are based on county production rather than unit production. The ACAT coverage is available at 65% of the yield coverage and 45% of the price coverage. The total cost for ACAT coverage is an administrative fee of $300, since its premium is fully subsidized. (Plastina, Current Crop Insurance Policies)

Crop Hail Insurance

In general, crop hail insurance provides protection against physical damage to the crop from hail or fire. It's strictly a yield based insurance tool with no contingencies for lost revenue resulting from any other loss. It's common for producers to purchase crop-hail insurance in conjunction with a MPCI policy. The strategy here is to help offset the MCPI deductible in the event of a covered disaster.

In the U.S. crop hail coverage is generally available from private insurers without any government subsidy. The reason for this is that hail is typically an isolated peril. It isn't associated with vast, widespread crop failures unlike other perils such as drought. Therefore, insurers are effectively able to spread their risk out by writing many policies across a wide geographical spectrum.

An assortment of riders can be attached to crop hail coverage including coverage for wind damage/**green snap**, as well as coverage for stored grain. Insurers also frequently offer discounts for early application and premium payment.

Again, crop insurance has a notoriously complex set of rules and stipulations that vary from one program to another and from one crop to another. In the short space I have allotted in this chapter, only simple terminology has been covered. I highly recommend discussing your options with a qualified crop insurance advisor. In any case, now that the basics of crop insurance have been covered, let's discuss some basic farm plans.

Calculating Loss Scenarios

The most important consideration a producer must make in evaluating his crop insurance options is this: how much loss can you afford? Clearly, every operation will answer this question differently. There is no one size fits all solution to insurance needs.

The answer to this question will guide you as you run some "what if" scenarios. Using your production and revenue estimates from Chapter 3 ask yourself what would happen if yields dropped by 10%? 20%? 50%? How much of a loss can you afford? Your insurance should cover at least that amount. When asking that question it's important to take into consideration your cash flow as well as any other sources of funding including savings that could offset the loss in whole or in part. Perhaps you might even be willing to consider a loan on your assets to cover a loss. If you're willing to cover some portion of a loss using your own funds, you are in effect, self insuring and may not need to pay for as much additional coverage as you thought.

Going through the scenarios is a relatively simple process. Simply multiply your expected harvested acreage times your expected yield for each crop you'll come up with your total production. Total production times the current market price you used in the revenue projection (Chapter 3) equals total projected revenue.

Total Revenue = (Harvested acres X Yield) Market price

Crop	Harvested Acres	Yield	Total Production (bu)	Market Price	Total Revenue
Soybeans	500	40	20,000	$10.50	$210,000

Once you have your total revenue projection, you can run through possible loss scenarios. Using our example from above, if total projected revenue from our soybean production is $210,000, what might happen if we sustained various losses? The formula is simple:

Total Revenue – (Total Revenue * %Loss)

For example, a scenario estimating revenue after a 10% production loss would be: $210,000- ($210,000 X 0.10) = $189,000

You can easily create a matrix of possible revenue outcomes using various potential losses. Below, there are revenue estimates for 10, 20 and 50% loss. I recommend you run through a number of different scenarios in order to ascertain not only your ability to sustain risk, but also your willingness to "**self insure.**" That is, how much risk are you willing to retain and cover using your own resources and not those of an insurance company?

10% Loss	25% Loss	50% Loss
$189,000.0	$157,500.0	$105,000.0

Another way to gain insight into insurance needs is to use historical information. If you've been in business for a number of years, look at the historical production of your farm. If you look back at your production history, how often do you experience below average yields? How often has your operation sustained a loss? The longer the historical period (data set) the more accurately you can estimate the significance of the next loss. If you don't have personal long term records, look for information elsewhere. County records can be a huge aid, particularly for beginning farmers with no production history on a given piece of ground.

It's also likely that lenders will require certain minimum coverage on your crop, both in the ground and in storage. You'll need to check with them for specifics but remember to treat their standards as a minimum; lenders are looking out for their own best interest. Minimum insurance simply to make a lender whole in the event of a covered loss may do very little to sustain the viability of your operation.

The goal of this chapter was simply to introduce some of the concepts and calculations that come up when making crop insurance decisions. With this basic information in hand, you'll have an easier time discussing your options with your insurance advisor and, just as importantly you are now a step closer to incorporating crop insurance into your overall marketing plan.

5 MANAGING BASIS RISK

During my years in the grain industry, I have routinely seen mass producer selling during futures market rallies. An up day in the market will typically see significantly more farmer selling than a down day. Conversely, there have been plenty of times where, as an export merchant, I have pushed my basis bids significantly higher and seen no farmer marketing. Now, I'm not suggesting these are necessarily incorrect marketing decisions, but it seems that many people think only of futures prices when it comes to marketing their grain.

Futures prices are much more publicized, and typically make up the bulk of the net flat price of a cash grain contract. Futures are unquestionably the sexier side of the market. However, farmers that are savvy marketers generally have a very good sense of where basis levels (sometimes referred to as premiums) are as well as directional trends in basis. This chapter will attempt to illustrate how basis levels are determined and, how you can use basis to your advantage.

Basis is, quite simply the difference between the flat price and the futures price at a specific delivery point.

$$\text{Basis} = \text{Flat Price} - \text{Futures Price}$$

In theory, basis levels at deliverable warehouses for futures contracts should approach zero as the contracts approach expiration, a tendency known as "convergence". There has been some controversy over the last few years regarding the convergence mechanism that has led some futures exchanges to change their terms regarding storage in an effort to force convergence. For our purposes, we'll assume it's perfectly functioning but this is not simply an academic exercise; a good understanding of basis function will help you make money.

First, remember that futures markets aren't simply exchanges for trading paper. You could obtain warehouse receipts for physical corn stocks in Chicago by taking a long futures position and holding onto it. You could then sell your stocks into any market area you want. What will it cost to get there? An easy way to understand how freight impacts basis levels is to visualize concentric circles surrounding the delivery warehouse where your stocks are held (Kub). The further the destination is from the warehouse, the higher the freight cost to move your stocks. To reflect the higher freight cost, the more distant market should reflect a higher basis. Of course, this is an oversimplified example but it is a generally sound description. The same holds true for the bids you get at your local elevator. If you're growing corn in Missouri, your bid will be less at the local elevator than what it would be delivered to the export terminal down in the Gulf.

So, basis is the only way to accurately compare values from one region to another. The futures price is the same throughout the U.S, only the basis will vary from one market area to another. When you call your local elevator to obtain bids, be certain you get both basis and futures price quotes, particularly if you're calling while futures markets are open. This is you're only means of comparing bids at one elevator versus another. For example, say you contact elevator A who is bidding $3.50 for corn delivered to their terminal for March delivery. 20 minutes later, elevator B is bidding $3.55. You may be tempted to sell elevator B your corn because they have a better bid right? Not necessarily. If March corn futures have appreciated in that 20 minutes, you may still be able to get a better price out of elevator A.

If we re-arrange the above formula, we could say that:
Flat Price = Futures Price + Basis
Elevator A: $3.50 = $4.00 + (-.50CH)
Elevator B: $3.55 = $4.10 + (-.55CH)

At -50, elevator A is actually bidding a higher basis number so you may be able to call them back and obtain a higher flat price based on the currently higher futures:

Elevator A: $3.60 = **$4.10** + (-.50CH)

In a moving futures market, the basis bid is your only way to really compare prices from one elevator to another. Keep in mind, basis is also subject to change but it is generally not nearly as volatile as the futures market. In a normally functioning market, elevators will probably update their basis only once or twice per day.

How Basis Levels are Determined

The problem many growers run into is that because basis levels vary so much from one region to another, it is difficult to find general summaries of basis behavior in the same way that futures information can be found. It's a relatively easy thing to find opinions and historical price data for any grain futures contract. The same isn't true for basis; producers must build up their own bank of information and develop their own opinions, or solicit them from their local grain elevators. Surprisingly however, many country elevators won't even have a readily available database of historical basis numbers.

How are basis levels determined? Because the grain trade is a competitive mart, the easy answer is to say that the market establishes basis prices where buyer and seller come together. This is very true, but certainly an oversimplified definition. The fundamental factors of supply and demand are in a constant tug of war, pushing and pulling prices up and down. Though the futures market can influence basis prices by making flat prices more appealing and thus resulting in more purchasing from end users or more selling from farmers (basis movement is normally inversely related to futures price movement), there are many other factors that influence basis.

Because basis is such a regional component of grain price, it is determined semi-independently of the futures market, based on local supply and demand factors. In addition to the all encompassing "supply and demand", local basis levels also include transportation costs and storage costs as well as crop quality discounts or premiums and a margin for the country elevator.

Supply and Demand Factors

Supply and price are inversely related; all else being equal higher supplies translate to lower prices and lower supplies translate into higher prices. When the supply is greater, at harvest for example, basis levels are generally pressured lower. Thus, local and regional grain stocks can have major impacts on local basis levels. In the draw area map, you can see that Montana Hard Red Winter Wheat works primarily into the PNW export market. So, a huge crop in Texas will probably have little impact on local basis levels in Montana. Conversely, a small HRW crop in Washington may provide some support to premiums in Montana.

Figure 3-HRW regional draw area map.

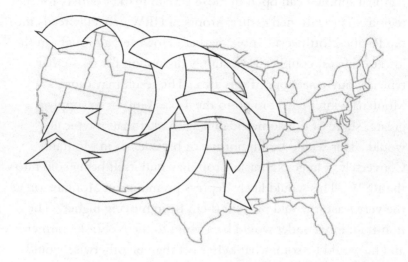

Another consideration is *when* the supply of grain is available. Just because production is big doesn't mean all of that grain is coming to market. We have run into a situation over the last several years where producers are holding large amounts of grain, right up until the last month before harvest. At that time, it becomes clear that they will have a marketable new crop and need to clear out bin space so they decide to once again start selling old crop grain. What happens to the basis? This situation is a case of a "pre harvest" glut (oversupply) of grain hitting the market all at once. Basis levels generally respond by moving lower in an attempt to ration the supply out over a longer period of time.

In times of oversupply, the market will typically price in a carry. Sean's rule of trading #5 is, if the market pays you to carry grain then carry it. If you find yourself in this situation, desperate to make space you clearly don't have the luxury of carrying grain. Additionally, you may be breaking rule #6 or some variation of it. The lesson here is this: Don't allow yourself to be forced into an unprofitable position.

Another consideration on supply side impact on basis is that regional supplies can open or close certain market outlets for that region. As mentioned earlier, Montana HRW generally feeds into the Pacific Northwest export market. However, a drought in the lower Midwest could cause a supply disruption for those that typically buy wheat out of this area. The result may cause Montana winter wheat to go to the Texas Gulf or to supply a greater share of the domestic milling market than it typically would. This would be supportive of basis levels in Montana. Conversely, a huge Nebraska crop may find itself being sold into the PNW. This would likely depress premiums in Montana or, at the very least it would prevent them from moving higher. The non-traditional outlet would be a boon to the Nebraska farmer and he would be somewhat better off than he otherwise would have. This is also another example of arbitrage; grain is forced into the most sensible channel until parity is restored to the market.

Finally, there is one last note regarding supply and demand. Grain demand can come from domestic and foreign buyers. Certain growing areas tend to work into specific regions very well as indicated by the HRW draw map. If Nigeria decides to increase their purchases, all else being equal this would be supportive for premiums at the Texas Gulf. Conversely, if demand out of the Gulf export market faltered, it would likely depress basis levels relative to other markets.

Transportation Factors

Differences in local basis levels are often largely the difference between freight rates from one point of origin to a various destinations. These include rail, barge and truck rates as well as fuel surcharges which have become common practice in recent years. Regardless of the conveyance, there is some cost associated with moving grain which is why grain elevators that are closer to final destinations typically have a higher basis than interior locations. Essentially, less of the basis price is being used to pay shipping costs. It's largely a function of freight rates.

An additional cost that is typically passed on to the farmer is the cost of freight in the secondary market. Essentially, commercial elevators have to pay for the right to load railcars or barges in addition to the published freight rate to move them to destination. Since there is a finite supply of rail freight, a market has developed where railcars are traded much like any other commodity. In recent years, the supply of rail freight has not been able to keep up with the demand. As a result, rail freight in this secondary market has spiked to levels as high as $7,000 per car on the BNSF railroad. If you're wondering, this is nearly $1.90 per bushel that a grain elevator must pay just for the right to load a train! Where does the elevator come up with that money? Well, that depends on the how the market is structured at any given time. Either the end user will end up paying for it in the form of higher prices or, it comes right out of the bid given to producers for their grain. The volatile freight market has presented some serious challenges to the marketplace and seriously distorted basis levels in the process. If you're a board member of a local coop, it would be prudent to insure that your company is accounting for these freight costs. It could mean the difference between liquidity and bankruptcy. If you're curious about freight costs in the secondary market, the USDA publishes information on the topic.

Local Competitiveness

One point that I keep mentioning over and over again is that the cash grain trade is a competitive mart. This is not only true on a macro level, where foreign buyers will choose to buy from the US or some other point of origin, but it is also true in a much more localized way. If you're lucky, you farm in an area with multiple buyers competing over your bushels. In general, the highest price in a trade area is likely to win your business (after your individual freight considerations of course). Each player in the market has different opinions, strategies and biases on price direction and some are probably willing to pay more than others during certain times.

Furthermore, this local competitiveness is also what spurs innovation and expansion at the country level. Grain elevators are in business to handle volume. So, the more grain they buy, the more opportunities they have to make money. Therefore, owners are sometimes willing to make investments to improve their ability to buy grain. This is why there has been a trend over the years toward more shuttle loading elevators. The cheaper freight rates mean they can pay you more in the form of higher basis and subsequently put more grain through the elevator.

Country grain elevators operate in an industry where margins are very uncertain. A surplus of available bushels will typically yield higher margins for local elevators. Conversely, crop failures cause extremely high competition for every kernel of grain and tend to compress margins. At the end of the day, if they're managed well a country elevator will take whatever the market will bear in terms of margins. The wider their margins, the lower your bid assuming all other factors are equal. Yet another reason that it's important to shop around for the best bid in the market.

Crop Quality

A final major factor in determining basis levels is crop quality. Really, this could fall into the supply and demand category but it has certain distinctions that make it important for producers to consider in making grain marketing decisions.

Imagine that North Dakota harvested a huge crop of hard red spring wheat. All else being equal, this should pressure basis levels lower. However, if the crop is extremely low protein, say 13% average, basis levels for the typical 14% hard red spring wheat may still be at historically high values. Since most demand for hard red spring wheat is for the higher protein, buyers will try to "pull" their desired quality through the supply chain. Its times like these that protein scales become incredibly wide, penalizing those with low protein and rewarding producers with higher protein.

The same scenario can be realized for virtually any grain crop during an off quality year. Markets become accustomed to specific grade specifications. End users become comfortable with certain qualities and are often reluctant to change them, even to the point of paying significant premiums for quality grain versus slightly off grade. This is particularly true for milling wheat but it is something to account for in all crops. The 2013 corn crop had major **aflatoxin** problems that resulted in huge discounts in the marketplace.

The Taiwan Flour Millers Association (TFMA) is a great example of a buyer being relatively unwilling to change their quality specifications for wheat tenders. Historically, TFMA has always purchases 13% protein HRW. Starting in 2010, protein levels in the HRW that was tributary to the PNW where Taiwanese boats were loaded became much lower. For years prior, 13% protein was relatively easy to source. In 2010 it became very difficult to come by. Despite premiums of $2.00 per bushel or more for proteins over 11.5 or 12.0% protein HRW, TFMA persisted in buying higher protein. Even lower priced alternatives such as 13% protein hard red spring wheat were usually not considered. So, the next time you see protein scales go off the rails, know that there is some buyer out there willing to pay the price.

Similarly, since many end users aren't willing to adjust their blends, off grade grain or low protein hard wheat may trade at a substantial discount. The demand for such products may not support the available supply.

Using Basis

All of this knowledge about where basis comes from is worthless if you can't put it to use in your own grain marketing decisions. Basis is a dynamic component of grain markets that warrants more consideration than many producers give it. It is critical for you to develop your own database of basis levels in your area so you can have a historical perspective. What constitutes a high basis? What would be a low basis? These numbers will be unique to your region. A good place to start is the USDA Agricultural Marketing Service (AMS).

This is the official USDA Market News basis report for soft red winter wheat delivered to the Gulf export market. It is sometimes reported with only a net price, so you'll have to subtract out the closing futures price in order to determine the applicable basis. Start compiling a spreadsheet of your own so you can look back at historical basis numbers.

Figure 4- USDA AMS Sample Market Report

Louisiana Midday bids and basis for US 2 Soft Red Winter Wheat

Cash Bids	Change	Basis	Change
Jun=6.25-6.31	up 4-dn 8	+44N to +50N	up 9-dn 3
Jul=6.25-6.27	up 4-dn 5	+44N to +46N	up 9-unch
Aug=6.29-6.31	dn 2-dn 3	+38U to +40U	up 3-2
Sep=6.36-6.41	dn 4-dn 0	+45U to +50U	up 1-5
Oct=6.71-6.76	dn 5	+60Z to +65Z	unch
Nov=6.71-6.76	dn 5	+60Z to +65Z	unch

Source: (USDA AMS)

Notice that prices are reported A) for a specific delivery period. In the example above, bids are provided for June through November. B) Basis is reported over a specific futures contract N for July, U for September and Z for December. We'll discuss these codes in the chapter on hedging with futures.

Note that the AMS also provides local numbers as well for an array of regions in each state. The numbers might not be spot on, but they should be close to actual market bids. Make use of this free resource; find your region and start tracking.

In your marketing plan you'll include historically high basis levels and historically low basis levels as a reference. Obviously, the market can take prices anywhere but it's useful to have an approximation of realistic values as a reference to point out opportunities. Many times in my career as a basis trader I would sell the basis simply because the values were relatively attractive compared to where they tended to be historically.

Transportation Considerations

So you've called around, found the best price and you're ready to sell your grain. Not so fast! You need to consider the actual cost of moving grain from your bin site, to the grain terminal. Using the example from the beginning of this chapter, suppose that elevators A and B are competing for your business.

Elevator A: $3.60 = $4.10 + (-.50)
Elevator B: $3.55 = $4.10 + (-.55)

All else being equal, Elevator A has the better price. But, it may not be the best price for you. You need to do one last calculation to determine which location will offer you the best return. If it costs you 25 cents/bushel to haul grain to Elevator A and only 15 cents/bushel to haul to Elevator B then Elevator B is actually the more profitable alternative.

Flat Price – Transportation Cost = Net Return
Elevator A: $3.60 - .25 = $3.35
Elevator B: $3.55 - .15 = $3.40

To determine your own transportation costs, you'll need to calculate fuel and labor costs on a per mile basis. Fuel and labor are relatively easy calculations. For fuel, all you need is an MPG estimate for your truck and the current fuel price per gallon. The formula is simple:

Fuel price per gallon/Vehicle MPG = Fuel cost per mile

Labor costs are equally simple to estimate. You simply need an estimate of how long the haul will likely take including loading and unloading and the hourly wage of your driver. The formula looks like this:

(#hours X hourly wage)/# of miles = labor cost per mile

From there, simply multiply the number of miles traveled (both ways) with your net cost per mile. Divide that figure by the number of bushels your truck can haul and you will arrive at cost per bushel to haul to a given destination.

For example, if the total haul is 15 miles from your farm to the elevator and it takes 2 hours to complete the trip at a fuel cost of $3.00/gallon and a truck that gets 10 MPG. Assuming you pay your driver $10 per hour your net cost per mile would be:

Fuel = $3.00/10MPG = 30 cents/mile
Labor= (2 hours X $10 per hour)/15 miles = $1.63 per mile
Total cost per mile= $1.63+.30 = $1.93 per mile
If your truck holds 1,000 bushels, your per bushel cost is:

$$(\$1.93 \text{ X } 15)/1,000 = 2.895 \text{ cents per bushel}$$

Going through this exercise will allow you to make realistic comparisons between one elevator's bids versus another.

When it comes to freight, some markets routinely quote bids based on a delivery market that is different from their location. For example, in the PNW it isn't uncommon for country elevators to quote bids based on delivery to the Portland export market. It's up to the producer to subtract the applicable barge freight rate from the quoted price. The moral is this: always check to make sure you know what the actual delivery point is when collecting bids from buyers.

A last consideration when it comes to locking in basis levels is the tendency buyers have to price in a time value discount into their bids. The further out you wish to contract, the more uncertainty there is regarding fundamental factors that affect price. How much will the US produce next year? How much will the world produce? What will the demand side of the equation look like? Because of this uncertainty, buyers will bid low for grain as payment for the risk they are assuming. That doesn't necessarily mean it's a bad deal, but it should be scrutinized before locking in a price.

Discount Schedules

I've already talked a bit about some discounts you may see when marketing grain. Of the major US crops, wheat tends to have the most punitive discounts associated with it largely because flour millers demand quality grain to meet the needs of increasingly picky consumers. This doesn't mean that discounts can be ignored for other crops however.

It sometimes seems as though producers ignore discounts until after grain is sold, hauled and settled by the elevator book keeper. At that point, if their quality was off grade, the farmer looks at his settlement and is understandably irate at what's been removed from his check. The mistake he made is twofold: first, he must ask for a copy of the discount schedule before ever selling grain in the first place. Second, he needs to compare discount schedules from one elevator to another in order to accurately compare the bids he is being given and estimate the price he will receive for his grain.

It's important to note that discount schedules are subject to change without notice so you need to check them often. This is particularly true during harvest as the elevator is trying to ascertain the overall quality of the crop coming in.

Basis is a critical component of grain marketing. As a producer, you need to make yourself an expert and trade accordingly. Don't expect any gifts from your buyers but always insist on being treated fairly and market accordingly.

6 HEDGING GRAIN IN THE FUTURES MARKET

The most publicized and talked about component of grain marketing is the futures market. Every day, millions of bushels are bought and sold by a variety of participants ranging from farmers to hedge fund managers. An entire industry has been developed simply to observe and report on movements in futures prices. When regular folks hear about wheat prices going up or down, you can bet they're not talking about basis.

With grain prices as volatile as they have become, using futures as a hedging tool is not only more difficult, it is also more necessary. The wild price swings mean more risk for the unprotected; for those in the industry, knowledge of the futures market is essential to managing a successful business.

Futures Market Basics

A futures market is a competitive mart (sound familiar?) that deals in the future delivery of a specific commodity. Futures contracts are traded on an **exchange** for a specific time frame and a specific delivery point. Contracts are generally 5,000 bushels (there are also "mini," 1,000 bushel contracts that have much smaller trading volume) of a certain commodity with defined grade specifications applicable for delivery. Exchanges determine other rules and regulations to help facilitate transactions between buyers and sellers as well as provide a system to help resolve disputes which may arise during the course of trade.

Trades that take place on a commodity futures exchange are all processed through the exchange **clearinghouse.** The clearinghouse keeps records of all trades by collecting this information from all of the exchange members at the end of each trading day. Each and every contract that is traded is recorded and when a trader has offset his position by taking an opposite trade, the clearinghouse will cancel the trader's obligation. It is this mechanism that makes trading in futures contracts so seamless. The simplicity of only having to take an offsetting position with the clearinghouse allows traders to buy and sell easily; one does not have to search out the party they originally traded with in order to cancel a position. The clearinghouse also ensures that all traders have sufficiently capitalized margin accounts in order to preserve the integrity of the marketplace.

Futures contracts are not traded for delivery in every month of the year. Each commodity is traded for predetermined shipment periods (contract months). Delivery will be made on a futures contract once the contract expires. Each contract month, has a special symbol associated with it.

Table 1- Futures Month Codes

January: F	July: N
February: G	August: Q
March: H	September: U
April: J	October: V
May: K	November: X
June: M	December: Z

Delivery is a key component for the futures market to properly function. Though futures are often talked about as paper markets, it's important to understand that there is a legitimate, underlying physical asset. The exchange sets specific quality specifications and delivery points applicable to each commodity. Frequently, there are multiple delivery warehouses available for a specific contract, all of which are printed in the exchanges trade rules.

When you trade in futures you are in fact forward contracting for physical grain. So, the trader who carries a futures position has two choices when it comes to closing out his position. He can either offset the position by buying or selling an equal and opposite position, or he can deliver or take delivery. Most trades are simply offset but under certain market conditions, commercial traders will physically take delivery or "stop" grain. Generally, these are very large companies who are able to see a bigger portion of the market and identify arbitrage opportunities allowing them to profit from stopping grain. Additionally, they may in fact have positions in the delivery facilities so they have a direct knowledge of the quality of the grain in-store. Physical delivery is not advisable for most hedgers.

For corn, soybeans and all three wheat contracts traded on US exchanges, futures are traded in $\frac{1}{4}$ cent increments. Furthermore, each commodity generally has daily limits for price movements. For example, if the daily trading limit in soybeans is 60 cents per bushel and the July contract is up 60 cents, we say it is "locked limit up." It can't trade any higher until the following trading day. The purpose of these limits is to prevent major runs on a market during frenzied trading. Some exchanges allow for expanded limits the day after locking limit up or down. Despite this, it is possible for traders to have a pretty good idea of where the contract would be trading by following 'synthetic trades' in options contracts.

'Synthetics' allow traders to ascertain the market price when an exchange is locked limit up or down. By evaluating the change in options premiums, traders can come up with an approximation of the value of the underlying futures contract.

Your broker should be able to tell you where the market is trading synthetically when the market is locked.

Participants in a futures market can generally be divided into two groups: speculators and hedgers. Speculators are traders willing to take a position in the market in an attempt to profit on price movements. They provide liquidity to the market thereby contributing to improved price discovery for other traders. Hedgers are commercial grain traders, exporters, farmers and end users who use the market to manage price risk and protect against price volatility.

There has been a lot of debate in recent years about the proper role of speculators in a futures market, particularly after crude oil spiked to over $147 per barrel in 2008. Elected officials began a witch hunt that eventually placed the blame for expensive gasoline squarely on the shoulders of large speculators. The problem with this line of thinking is the notion that speculators are always on one side of a trade. Speculators can just as easily take a short position as a long position, and in fact they frequently do. What would a futures market look like without speculators? For one, volume would be much lower. Markets would be much less liquid and placing hedges would therefore become more of a challenge for hedgers.

If you want a good example, compare and contrast the Minneapolis wheat contract with the Chicago wheat contract. Minneapolis has speculative money to be sure, but the volume of speculators is substantially lower than it is in Chicago. In fact, in the January 13, 2015 Commitments of Traders Report, "managed money" had long positions of 82,721 contracts and short positions totaling 72,037 contracts in Chicago wheat. On the same day, Minneapolis had long positions of 8,225 contracts and short positions of 2,558 (CFTC). The difference is staggering. Which market is more liquid? Which typically has a much closer spread between the bids and offers? The answer to both questions is the Chicago contract. It should also be noted that on this particular day speculative funds have substantial long and short positions, meaning that various funds are providing both bids and offers in the market. If that's not adding liquidity, I don't know what is. In my opinion, speculative money is essential to the performance of the market.

All participants are required to have a certain percentage of the value of each contract in a special "margin account." Each commodity exchange determines what their margin requirements are and they are subject to change. A margin account must be deposited with a registered futures commission merchant, which can be set up by your broker. Typically, speculators are required to maintain a higher balance in their margin accounts than are hedgers.

Spreads

Commercial grain traders pay very close attention to the price spreads between various contracts. The most common (and most liquid) are intra-market spreads. An **intra-market spread** or calendar spread is simply the difference in price between various contract months of the same commodity. These are important to watch in order to understand price carries and inverses. Watching calendar spreads will tell you when to sell your grain.

Trading intra-market spreads simply involves buying one contract month and selling another. For example, a bull spread involves buying a nearby contract and selling a deferred contract. A bear spread is just the opposite; it involves selling a nearby contract and buying a deferred month. A trader initiating a spread trade is hoping to profit from movements in the difference between the two contracts. A bull spreader is betting that the nearby price will move higher relative to the deferred price and a bear spreader is betting that the deferred price will move higher relative to the nearby.

It's interesting to note that futures exchanges view intra-market spread trading to be a less risky proposition than outright long or short positions. This is because there is a tendency for contracts of the same commodity to move in tandem. If one contract month moves higher, generally they all move higher. So, your long position is offset by your short position, at least in part. Obviously, this isn't always true. If you grow Hard Red Spring wheat and hedge in Minneapolis you've seen the nearby futures month do some pretty crazy things relative to the other contract months. Still, since there is a general tendency for the prices to move in the same direction, futures exchanges will generally require a smaller upfront margin deposit for intra-market spread trades.

Calendar spreads are critical for grain marketers to understand and monitor. They can take on 3 different forms. Spreads can be priced at a **carry**, an **inverse** or they can be flat.

In a normal market, we'll see carries in calendar spreads. That is to say, a **deferred** month will be worth more than the nearby month. This reflects the costs of storing grain. Interest, depreciation and grain conditioning are all real costs borne by anybody in the business of storing grain. Naturally, you'd expect to be paid for that service. This is the function of market carries. Obviously, the marketplace isn't always willing to pay for this service. When grain is scarce or demand is particularly high, spreads will reflect the difference.

A flat or inverted (sometimes referred to as backwardated) market does not pay warehouseman to store grain. An inverse means that grain is worth more nearby than it is in deferred months. When calendar spreads are flat, or even more so when they are inverted, the market is signaling for those holding physical grain to sell the nearby month. See Sean's rules for grain marketing #3 and 4. Basically, do what the market signals you to do. Don't fight it; allow the market to work for you.

An inter-market spread is the price difference between two different commodities futures contracts. This could be the difference between corn and soybeans or hard red spring and hard red winter wheat. Oil processors will frequently trade crush spreads (soybeans/oil/meal), crude oil refiners will trade the crack spread (crude/gasoline/heating oil). Still, these players manage these spreads as hedges against their physical business. The more speculative crowd could trade spreads on virtually anything. For example, long corn short soybeans or long crude short soybeans. In any case, as a producer, you need to watch various inter-market price spreads in order to make informed planting decisions.

Margin

In general, commodity futures contracts don't require traders to fund the entire amount of their trade. Futures exchanges typically view futures trading as having limited short term risk. In other words, under normal circumstances we don't see 50-60 cent moves in a single day. So, the various exchanges have determined that only a portion of the total value of a trade needs to be funded at any given time. For example, say the total value of a 5,000 bushel corn contract is $20,000. A 20 cent move represents only $1,000.

There are two types of margin requirements which are imposed by the exchanges. These are the **initial margin** and the **maintenance margin.** The initial margin is the dollar amount that is required to be deposited with your brokerage at the time a trade is initiated. Using the above example, let's say you buy 1 corn contract. Even though the actual value is $20,000, you may only need to have $1,500 in your margin account.

The maintenance margin requirement kicks in when your positions start working against you. Let's say that corn futures drop by $0.25/bushel from $4.00 to $3.75. The value of your margin account also drops from 1,500 to $250. If the maintenance margin requirement is $1,000, you will be required to immediately deposit an additional $750 into your margin account.

Though minimum margin requirements are set by the exchange, individual brokerage houses are free to demand more than the minimum requirement. They may not waive or reduce the minimum margin requirement however. Occasionally, futures exchanges will change the minimum requirements as the value of the underlying contract changes. A higher priced commodity, soybeans for example, will have a higher margin requirement than a lower priced commodity such as corn.

The fact that commodities futures are traded on margin means that they are **leveraged**. In other words, the risk/reward of trading futures is more than what you've put up in your margin account. Of course, for hedgers this isn't as significant as it is for speculators since we have offsetting positions but it's still important to take note of.

What is Hedging?

The definition of hedging is to take an equal but opposite position in the cash and futures market. Since grain growers are generally long cash grain, in order to hedge your position you would need to sell futures. It works like this:

Let's say for example that you have 40,000 bushels of soybeans in bins on your farm. By selling 8 contracts (40,000 bushels) of soybean futures, you are "perfectly hedged." That is, all of your grain is protected against futures price drops. Subsequently, you won't be able to take advantage of futures price rallies either. The following table illustrates possible outcomes if you hedged at a futures price of $11.50.

Grain Price	Un-hedged Gain/Loss	Hedged Gain/Loss
$10.50	$-40,000.00	$0.00
$11.00	$-20,000.00	$0.00
$11.50	0.00	$0.00
$12.00	$20,000.00	$0.00
$12.50	$40,000.00	$0.00

By hedging when the market is at $11.50 you prevent future losses if market prices move lower. Again, you will also be unable to take advantage of price rallies the way an un-hedged cash position would be able to. Also, remember that hedging your position using the futures market leaves the basis portion of the flat price un-hedged so you will still be exposed to fluctuations in basis levels. A futures hedge does not constitute a cash contract.

At some point, you will want to enter into a cash contract with a local elevator to physically handle your grain. At that point, you would need to "unwind" your hedge by buying futures of the same contract month and commodity as your existing hedges. You will recognize either a gain or loss on your futures trade that will be offset by the gain or loss on your new cash contract.

To expand on the earlier example, let's say you hedge 40,000 bushels of soybeans in the futures market at $11.50 per bushel. If at the time you decide to write a cash contract with your local elevator the market has dropped to $10.50, you will have a gain in your futures account of $40,000. However, this will be offset by the lower price you received on your cash contract.

Grain Price	Futures gain/loss	Cash gain/loss
$10.50	$40,000.00	-$40,000.00
$11.00	$20,000.00	-$20,000.00
$11.50	**$0.00**	**$0.00**
$12.00	-$20,000.00	$20,000.00
$12.50	-$40,000.00	$40,000.00

For hedged grain, at each and every futures price there will be a gain or a loss that will be offset by a corresponding gain or loss on the cash contract. This can be illustrated graphically as follows:

Figure 1- Breakeven Illustration for hedged grain

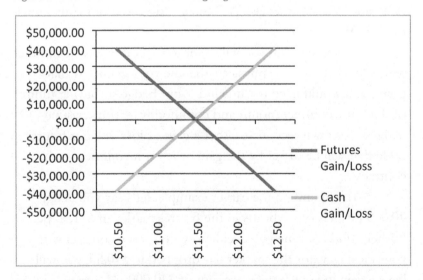

This example assumes that you lift your short hedge at the same price as the cash sale. In order to simplify the process most commercial traders will exchange futures contracts with one another at the time of a cash sale. Also known as a "versus cash" this transaction is facilitated by the futures brokers of both companies and allows for a seamless transfer of futures at prices agreeable to both companies. Most grain elevators will be able to accommodate you should you wish to exchange futures with them when you sell cash grain.

Essentially, when you enter into a cash contract with a grain elevator, they would "give" futures to you. You would "take" them at a price level equivalent to the cash contract. Your "take" of futures would offset your short hedge on the futures exchange thus zeroing out your futures position.

As noted earlier, futures contracts are traded for specific contract months, not every month of the year. For this reason, it may be a bit confusing to know which contract is appropriate to use for placing your hedge. This will largely depend on the time frame you would like to use for actually delivering your grain to market. In general, you will want to select the futures month that is nearest to your desired shipment period but not prior to it. For example, if you wanted to sell cash corn for January, February or March delivery you would hedge using March futures. For April delivery, you would hedge using May futures. By hedging in the appropriate month, you will avoid taking risk on calendar spreads.

When to lift a hedge

Generally, you will lift your hedge (buy back a short hedge or sell a long hedge) at the same time you enter into a contract for physical delivery. It is often convenient to do a "futures exchange" with the other contracting party as explained in the previous section. Your broker will arrange to swap futures between the counterparties. If an exchange isn't possible, you can simply enter an offsetting trade in the futures market to lift your hedge.

There are times when it may be advisable to lift a hedge before the sale of physical grain takes place. One reason would be to avoid carrying a position into "delivery." Delivery is the time period of a futures contract where positions are locked into physically taking ownership or delivering stocks at a registered delivery warehouse. Obviously for most of us, this is not something we want to do as it can be a costly process even for those who routinely participate.

A second reason to lift a hedge before a cash sale would be to take advantage of a market carry. If you sold July futures as a hedge against physical grain and three months later, the carry has widened from 10 to 20 cents going into the September contract, it may be advisable to lift your July hedge.

In either of these circumstances **"rolling"** your short hedge forward may be the best option. Rolling is a simple way to maintain your hedge while simultaneously earning the carry or delaying physical sales. A roll would involve taking in offsetting position in the nearby contract while at the same time re-establishing your hedge in the September contract. If you're carrying a short hedge as most producers will be, you would buy back July and sell September. The spread can be independently traded without having to put two separate orders. For example, you could place a limit order with your broker to buy July and sell September at a 20 cent carry. This will ensure the best possible fill.

Types of futures orders

The two types of orders I placed most frequently as a trader and the types that you are most likely to use are **limit orders** and **market orders**. A limit order is a directive to buy or sell at a specific price. You've got a figure in mind where you want to hedge your long cash corn position, say $5.00. You would call your broker (or enter electronically) and instruct them to sell 1 CZ at $5.00. Limit orders are not guaranteed a fill since there is a chance that the market doesn't reach the $5.00 mark. In fact, you're not guaranteed a fill unless CZ trades *through* $5.00. That is to say, you wouldn't know for sure that your order was filled unless CZ traded at least at $5.0025. The reason for this is that there could be numerous orders to sell at $5.00. If there are 100 contracts offered at $5.00 and only 1 contract trades there, there are 99 others that did not fill despite the fact that the market actually traded at your desired price.

Market orders on the other hand are always filled at the best possible bid or ask. In the above example, if the bid is $4.99 and you put in a market order to sell 1 CZ, you'll be filled at $4.99. Your order is guaranteed to fill but not necessarily at the price you'd hoped for. Market orders are great in a very liquid market but when the bid and offer become wide, as sometimes happens in Minneapolis, you'll want to use caution before entering a market order. This is particularly true if it's for a sizeable quantity. How is this possible? Well, if there are 2 contracts bid at $5.00 and 3 at $4.96, a relatively small market order to sell 5 contracts could move the market price by 4 cents or more. Imagine what an order to sell 100 contracts might do.

Other order types include **stops** (or stop loss), **stop limit, market if touched,** and **market on open (close).** A stop order is generally used to exit a position either to prevent further losses or to protect profits. It is sometimes used to initiate a new position if the trader feels that breaking through a support or resistance level indicates a change in trend. In the case of our short hedge, a stop order would be placed to sell 1 CZ *below* the current market price. For example, if CZ is currently trading at $5.10 and we want to protect ourselves from further downside risk if it trades below $5.01, we could place $5.00 stop. If the market hits $5.00 our stop order converts to a market order and will fill at the best possible price.

A stop limit order is very similar to a basic stop order, but instead of converting to a market order when the specified level is reached, it becomes a limit order. Like a regular limit order, we are not guaranteed a fill but if our order does fill, it will be at $5.00 or better.

A market if touched (MIT) is the opposite of a stop order. In the case of our $5.00 sell target, if CZ is currently trading at $4.90, we can enter an MIT order. If the market touches $5.00, our order converts to a market order and we'll receive the best possible fill.

The market on open/close order types are used when we want to get the best possible fill during the open or close of the market. We're not guaranteed to obtain the actual settlement price but it will likely be something close to it. As a trader I never once personally utilized this type but it can be useful during frenzied markets if you've got strong directional bias.

All of these order types can be for any length of time. Typically, **day orders**, **good til cancelled (GTC)** or **fill or kill** are used to place a futures order. A day order is pretty straight forward. If we enter an order at any time during the trading day, it will expire at the close. Obviously this doesn't apply to market orders which are immediately filled.

GTC orders are generally stop or limit orders that are way out of the market. It's convenient to simply leave them "open" with our broker so that we don't have to constantly monitor the price; we pay our broker for that. A GTC order remains in force until it is filled or cancelled, whichever comes first. A word of caution: don't place a GTC order and forget it. I've been filled on orders during the delivery period when the market is much less liquid and had to pay dearly to get out. Of course, you'll want to cancel them before that happens.

Finally, the fill or kill order. As the market becomes more and more electronically traded, this type of order is fading in use. Essentially, it's a "get it done now, or don't do it at all" type of limit order. We would call our broker with our order to sell 1 CZ at $5.00. She would offer the order 3 times and only 3 times. If the market didn't respond she would return to us with an "unable" and the order would be cancelled.

A good working knowledge of the futures market is critical for a successful grain marketer. It is a significant part of your business and therefore one that you should take very seriously. I recommend purchasing a subscription to a service that provides live streaming quotes, historical data and charting tools. It will cost a couple hundred dollars per month but its chump change compared to making a few extra pennies per bushel on your overall production.

7 USING OPTIONS TO IMPROVE YOUR MARGINS

I've found that one of the most underutilized tools for managing price risk that is currently at the disposal of farmers are options contracts. Perhaps that's because they can be confusing. Perhaps it's because they aren't a critical component to creating a cash grain contract. Still, the fact that they are underutilized is disappointing. Options can help you improve margins on your grain sales and increase the profitability of your farm.

Farmers are generally very familiar with the concept and use of insurance in their operations. You buy all sorts of insurance coverage to protect various assets in the event that some unforeseen event causes damage and the cost is more than you can bear. In order to justify purchasing, the cost of an insurance policy must be relatively affordable compared with the potential loss if you didn't buy insurance. Electing not to purchase insurance is also known as self-insuring.

Options are not unlike insurance policies on price risk. I would guess that you pay a lot more time scrutinizing the daily movements in grain futures than you do thinking about whether your combine will roll off a cliff. Which would you say poses a greater risk to the profitability of your operation? Most farmers would say price risk is more significant, yet I would bet that most farmers buy insurance to protect their combine but not to protect against price risk. Options provide a way for you to insure against drops in prices *and* take advantage of futures price appreciation.

Options Basics

An option is a **derivative** of a futures contract. In other words, an option derives its value based on the value of the underlying futures contract. An options contract affords the owner the right but not the obligation to go long or short at a specific **strike** price. A **call** option gives the owner the right to buy futures at the set strike price. A **put** option gives the owner the right to sell futures at the set strike price. To purchase an option, the buyer pays a premium to the **option writer** in exchange for taking on the price risk. In the event the owner decides to exercise his or her option to buy or sell futures, the option seller, or writer takes an opposing position in the underlying futures contract.

All options contract have a specific **expiration** date. This is the day where, if an option hasn't been exercised, it will expire worthless. Throughout the life of an option, it will be described by traders as either **in the money, at the money, or out of the money**. An option is at the money when the strike price is the same as the corresponding futures price. A call is out of the money when the strike price is higher than the corresponding futures price and in the money when the strike price is lower than the corresponding futures price. A put option is out of the money when the strike price is lower than the corresponding futures price and it is in the money when the strike price is higher than the corresponding futures.

The price you pay to purchase an option is called the option **premium.** Premiums are established in a competitively traded marketplace that is separate and distinct from the futures market. There are several price components included in the option premium.

First of all, an option has **time value**. That is, the further away from expiration in option is, the higher its value. As an option approaches expiration it experiences **time decay.** In other words, the premium drops as the option gets closer to expiring. This is because there is less time risk associated with selling a short term option. Imagine that you sell a call option with a $7.50 strike price. If there is one year remaining on the option contract the odds that the option is exercised are higher than if there was only 1 week remaining. For this reason, option writers demand a higher price for longer term options. This is the time value.

Option premiums also have an **intrinsic value** priced into them. The intrinsic value of an option is simply the money that could be pocketed by immediately exercising the instrument. So, only options that are currently in the money actually have any intrinsic value. Again, for put options this is when the strike price is greater than the current underlying futures price. Calls are in the money when the strike price is less than the current futures price.

Since option premiums are made up of time value and intrinsic value, the total option premium should be the sum of the two. In theory this is true; on an options expiration day, the premium should be equal to the intrinsic value. However, since options are traded in a competitive auction, this isn't always the case. Sophisticated options traders at major trading houses use computer models to ascertain theoretical premiums and determine whether a specific option should be bought or sold.

Among some of the more commonly used tools they utilize are a number of 'Greeks.' These figures are readily available to anybody who is paying for a futures quote or service. Greeks include a number of mathematically derived figures that were designed to provide indications on buying and selling opportunities in options trading. They include delta, gamma, theta and vega.

The options **delta** is used to measure risk. The delta measures the movement in an option premium given a specific unit change in the underlying futures price and it is the most widely used figure in options trading but there are other "Greeks" that traders use. **Gamma** measures how fast the delta changes as the underlying futures contract changes. **Theta** measures the rate at which an options' time value decreases. Finally, **Vega** measures the overall riskiness of the market. As you become more educated on options strategies, you'll want to learn more about these figures.

Using Options

So, we've established that options are much like an insurance contract. They are traded in an open market with buyers and sellers looking to transfer risk, at a price called an option premium. Options give the owner, the right but not the obligation to take a position in the underlying futures contract at the option strike price. Now, we will take a closer look at what options can do to help you manage price risk and increase operating margins for your farm.

Options prices are generally reported in one of two ways. Either tables with specific strike prices across a range of expirations or specific expirations with a range of strike prices. The table below shows September Corn options on 6/20/2014.

Table 1- Option Strike Price Snapshot

CALLS

Strike Price	Volume	High	Low	Prior Settle	Change	Last
395	0	-	-	30'1	-	-
400	0	-	25'5	26'6	-1'1	25'5
405	0	-	-	23'5	-	-

410	1	20'4	19'7	20'6	-0'7	19'7
415	0	-	-	18'2	-	-
420	8	15'2	14'4	16'0	-1'4	14'4
425	0	-	-	14'0	-	-
430	0	-	11'3	12'2	-0'7	11'3
435	0	-	10'0	10'5	-0'5	10'0
440	0	-	8'5	9'2	-0'5	8'5

PUTS

Strike Price	Last	Change	Prior Settle	Low	High	Volume
395	6'4	+0'1	6'3	-	6'4	0
400	8'2	+0'2	8'0	8'0	8'2	2
405	10'2	+0'3	9'7	-	10'2	0
410	12'5	+0'4	12'1	12'5	12'5	8
415	15'2	+0'6	14'4	-	15'2	0
420	18'0	+0'6	17'2	-	18'0	1
425	20'4	+0'2	20'2	-	20'4	0
430	23'6	+0'3	23'3	-	23'6	11
435	27'1	+0'2	26'7	-	27'1	0
440	30'6	+0'2	30'4	29'5	30'6	2

Each strike price has a corresponding row of data. For example, a put option with a strike price of $4.20 last traded at 18 cents. Options are traded in 1/8 cent increments so the +0'6 increase equates to a ¾ of a cent increase in the premium. The previous day's settlement was 17'2 or 17 ¼ cents. The High and Low prices for the day are listed only if there are trades. Because there are such a large array of options choices in different strike prices and expirations, the volume for any one contract tends to be relatively low when compared with the underlying futures contract.

Options Strategies for Producers

Options contracts provide producers with marketing flexibility that flat price trading simply cannot offer. They can provide the ability to hedge against price risk while maintaining the opportunity to benefit from price rallies. Additionally, they can provide flexibility and protection against reduced yields on forward contracted grain.

Buying Puts

Incorporating options strategies into your overall marketing plan doesn't have to be complicated. While there a number of more sophisticated systems that are used by some options traders, for the average hedger it can be as simple as buying a put. In fact, buying puts is a great place to start for our purposes. As a pure insurance policy, it's easy to illustrate:

Table 1- Comparison of outcomes for long put strategy

(Basis = 0)

March futures	Buy a $5.50 Put for 35 cents	Hedge at $5.50	Do Nothing
$5.00	$5.15	$5.50	$5.00
$5.10	$5.15	$5.50	$5.10
$5.20	$5.15	$5.50	$5.20
$5.30	$5.15	$5.50	$5.30
$5.40	$5.15	$5.50	$5.40
$5.50	$5.15	$5.50	$5.50
$5.60	$5.25	$5.50	$5.60
$5.70	$5.35	$5.50	$5.70
$5.80	$5.45	$5.50	$5.80
$5.90	$5.55	$5.50	$5.90
$6.00	$5.65	$5.50	$6.00

The put option acts as an insurance policy for downside price risk. As you can see, your price risk is limited to the option premium (plus any applicable brokerage fees). So, you can effectively mitigate price risk while at the same time retain the opportunity to take advantage of futures market rallies. Hedgers would implement this strategy when they are bearish or uncertain on futures price direction. (Iowa State University)

The trouble with this strategy in recent years has been the high cost of put options. As a derivative, options contracts are sensitive to movements in the underlying instrument (the futures contract). The high volatility in the futures market has resulted in options writers to price in a greater risk premium into the price of the option contract. The end result is hedgers can be priced out of the market when it comes to buying this type of insurance policy. They have their place however, and buying puts shouldn't be ignored as a possible strategy.

Writing Puts

If premiums for puts are too high for a hedger to want to buy, what about writing puts?

Table 2- Comparison of outcomes for short put strategy

(Basis = 0)

March futures	Write a $5.50 Put for 35 cents	Hedge at $5.50	Do Nothing
$5.00	$4.85	$5.50	$5.00
$5.10	$4.95	$5.50	$5.10
$5.20	$5.05	$5.50	$5.20
$5.30	$5.15	$5.50	$5.30
$5.40	$5.25	$5.50	$5.40
$5.50	$5.85	$5.50	$5.50
$5.60	$5.95	$5.50	$5.60
$5.70	$6.05	$5.50	$5.70

$5.80	$6.15	$5.50	$5.80
$5.90	$6.25	$5.50	$5.90
$6.00	$6.35	$5.50	$6.00

The above scenario is assuming that you write a cash contract for your grain at the corresponding futures price. So, if you contract your grain at $5.00 you would end up with a net price of $4.85/bushel by writing the put as illustrated. This price is obtained as follows:

Option Premium-(Market Price- Strike Price) +Market Price
$0.35+ ($5.00-$5.50) +$5.00 = $4.85

This strategy would be employed as a "margin enhancer" during times when you are bullish futures. You keep the option premium (less any applicable brokerage fees) but your downside risk is large. In theory, if the underlying futures price went to zero, you'd suffer a big loss. As a general rule, writing puts is not my favorite options strategy for producers but it can present opportunities for savvy marketers.

Buying Calls

Call options can also be very appealing choices for grain marketers. For example, the minimum price contract available at many grain elevators utilizes call options to lock in a price floor. For hedgers, the strategies aren't all that different from writing or buying puts. Call options however, offer some distinct differences.

As mentioned above, going long a call option can effectively establish a minimum price for your grain while simultaneously allowing the opportunity to profit from price appreciation. Obviously this opportunity comes at a price; the option premium (plus any applicable brokerage fees).

Table 3- Comparison of outcomes for long call strategy

(Basis = 0)

March futures	Buy a $5.50 Call for 35 cents	Hedge at $5.50	Do Nothing
$5.00	**$5.15**	$5.50	$5.00
$5.10	**$5.15**	$5.50	$5.10
$5.20	**$5.15**	$5.50	$5.20
$5.30	**$5.15**	$5.50	$5.30
$5.40	**$5.15**	$5.50	$5.40
$5.50	**$5.15**	$5.50	$5.50
$5.60	$5.25	$5.50	$5.60
$5.70	$5.35	$5.50	$5.70
$5.80	$5.45	$5.50	$5.80
$5.90	$5.55	$5.50	$5.90
$6.00	$5.65	$5.50	$6.00

This example assumes that you enter into a cash contract with your local elevator at a futures price of $5.50 per bushel. Since you paid 35 cents for the call option, your net price is $5.15 per bushel. Notice that the lowest cash price you can get for your grain under this scenario is $5.15 per bushel. However, if the futures price appreciates during the life of the option, you can take advantage of those price increases by exercising or selling your call.

Writing Calls

One of my favorite options strategies for producers is simply writing covered calls. Not only is it an easy way to improve your margins, it's also simple. That's not to say it's without risks but you can protect yourself. The key is to choose your strike prices wisely. You'll want to select strikes that have a high probability of resulting in correspondingly profitable cash sales.

Table 4-Comparison of outcomes for short call strategy

(Basis = 0)

March futures	Write a $5.50 Call for 35 cents	Hedge at $5.50	Do Nothing
$5.00	$5.35	$5.50	$5.00
$5.10	$5.45	$5.50	$5.10
$5.20	$5.55	$5.50	$5.20
$5.30	$5.65	$5.50	$5.30
$5.40	$5.75	$5.50	$5.40
$5.50	$5.85	$5.50	$5.50
$5.75	$5.85	$5.50	$5.60
$6.00	$5.85	$5.50	$5.70
$6.50	$5.85	$5.50	$5.80
$7.00	$5.85	$5.50	$5.90
$7.50	$5.85	$5.50	$6.00

This could actually be illustrated to show large losses as the March futures price appreciates. Consider that you will be taking a short position at $5.50 even if the futures price is $7.50. In theory, that's a $2.00 loss. On paper, that's true. But don't forget the idea behind this strategy. It's a margin enhancer. You wrote the option under the assumption that a $5.50 cash sale was profitable for your enterprise and you pocketed a 35 cent premium; (that's the bonus margin). So, though you lose out on the opportunity to profit from the price appreciation, you still protect yourself by entering into a profitable trade and pocketing an extra 35 cents.

The risk here is that the futures price drops. There is no minimum price under this scenario, at least not one worth considering (in reality, if the price went to zero your floor would be 35 cents).

Buy a Put and Sell a Call

In addition to the relatively simple options trades described above, there are also a number of more complex strategies. Let's say that you like the idea of establishing a minimum price on a forward contract but that the cost of buying a call option is simply too expensive for you. One option is to offset the cost of purchasing an option, buy writing an offsetting option:

Table 5- Comparison of outcomes for long put/short call strategy

Long 8.50 put (.30 premium), short 8.75 call (.20 premium)

Sep Futures	Basis	Put Gain (Loss)	Call Gain (Loss)	Net Price
$7.50	($0.25)	$0.70	$0.20	$8.15
$7.75	($0.25)	$0.45	$0.20	$8.15
$8.00	($0.25)	$0.20	$0.20	$8.15
$8.25	($0.25)	($0.05)	$0.20	$8.15
$8.50	($0.25)	($0.30)	$0.20	$8.15
$8.75	($0.25)	($0.30)	$0.20	$8.40
$9.00	($0.25)	($0.30)	($0.05)	$8.40
$9.25	($0.25)	($0.30)	($0.30)	$8.40
$9.50	($0.25)	($0.30)	($0.55)	$8.40

This strategy is known as a "fence." It utilizes offsetting positions to essentially create a range of selling prices depending on where the underlying futures market is trading. In practice, you'd probably select a strategy that would afford higher upside potential. In that scenario, the net cost to you would be higher but the upside price potential would also be higher.

To calculate the selling price range you would use the following formulas:

Floor Price=
Put Strike price- put premium + call premium+ expected basis

Ceiling Price=
Call Strike price-put premium + call premium + expected basis

The key to this strategy is to select a selling price that reflects a profitable trade for your business. It can be used in conjunction with a basis fixed contract if you want to remove basis risk from the equation.

Realizing Options Gains and Losses

There are 3 ways to exit an options position and recognize your gain or loss. You can enter an offsetting position, the option can be **exercised** or, it can expire.

More often than not, options positions are exited by buying or selling an equal and opposite position of an identical option, thus offsetting the position. There are two main reasons for this. First, the only way for an option owner to maintain any time value is to sell his position before the option reaches expiration. Remember, at expiration, the time value equals zero. Second, in order to avoid being assigned a futures position (exercised against), you must liquidate your position.

If an option is exercised, this means that it has been converted into the underlying futures contract and both parties are assigned their relative positions. For example, if you purchased a Sep call option at $6.50 and decide to exercise your right on the option you will go long 1 contract of Sep futures at $6.50 regardless of where the current instrument is trading. So, if it is currently at $7.00, you will own 1 contract at $6.50 and the option writer will be short at $6.50. In order to avoid carrying into delivery, the futures positions will then need to be offset. The long position will realize a 50 cent gain and the short position will realize a 50 cent loss on the futures portion.

Finally, an option can simply expire. Options buyers have the right to do nothing. In this case, the option will expire worthless. The option buyer is out no more than his initial premium and the option seller retains the entire premium as profit.

Instituting an options strategy into your overall grain marketing plan can be a good way to mitigate risk, or an opportunity to improve your overall returns. Options' trading is not without its risk, particularly if you are writing the contracts. It's important that you consider your own tolerance for risk when developing an option strategy.

8 FORECASTING GRAIN PRICE MOVEMENTS

In 2010, a study by Professors Christopher Chabris of Union College and Daniel Simons of the University of Illinois conducted a study that has come to be known as 'The Invisible Gorilla Study.' Participants were shown a video of several people playing basketball and were asked to count the number of times the ball was passed from one player to another. Right in the middle of the video, an individual in a gorilla suit walks into the middle of the frame, waves and walks out. Seems pretty obvious right? Interestingly, roughly half of study participants never saw the gorilla. The findings suggest that people can become so focused on one thing that they neglect other obvious events (Chabris and Simons).

Price forecasting is an art and a very imperfect one at that. It's easy to get caught up in relatively insignificant, small picture clues when there are frequently much more important indicators to monitor. Still, any grain trader worth his salt will work hard at evaluating the market in order to develop an opinion on price direction. In fact, there are traders out there who get paid a lot of money to be right *some* of the time. The key for them and you is to be right more often than they're wrong. To do that, they need to sift through the unimportant information in order to find the truly valuable insights. The truth is nobody is correct 100% of the time but, if you want to be a successful grain marketer, you *must* form an opinion.

Up to this point the concepts in this book have asked you to make assumptions on prices; in the next chapter when we discuss putting together your marketing plan you'll need to utilize the skills discussed in this chapter in order to make those assumptions.

As a general rule, price forecasting techniques will fit into one of two categories: **fundamental analysis** and **technical analysis**. Fundamental analysis involves researching and evaluating hard data. That hard data can come from any number of sources including government statisticians and private information sources but, it always comes down to estimating supply and demand figures. Technical analysis isn't nearly as black and white. It involves the evaluation of price trends usually in the form of charts in an effort to predict future price changes.

There are countless books, articles and various electronic resources out there that go into great depth on price forecasting. In this chapter, I'll focus only on the basics of the art. Additionally, I'll tell you where to find commodity specific information to aid you in evaluating the markets that are relevant to you. For further study, I recommend Jack Schwager's Technical and Fundamental analysis books.

The Efficient Markets Hypothesis

There's a joke that every economist in the world has either told or heard at least once. Two economists are walking down the sidewalk when they come upon a $20 bill lying on the ground. One of them bends down to pick it up and the other says to him, 'Don't bother, if there really were a $20 bill sitting on the ground, somebody would have picked it up already.' The idea is that as soon as there is some piece of information available to the marketplace, prices will have taken this information into account. In other words, market prices always reflect all available information. It may seem silly, particularly using the story of the two economists. However, this notion is a very hotly debated one within the world of academic economists.

Why bring this idea up here? Frankly, if the efficient markets hypothesis is true, wasting one's time in attempting to forecast prices is a completely foolish endeavor. The point is this: markets are not completely efficient; they're imperfect when it comes to digesting information. There are many players involved in trading grain, each with access to some similar information and some information that is unique to them.

As I mentioned earlier, there are traders out there who are paid a great deal of money to outguess the market and much of that money is well earned. Yes, the market assimilates information quickly. It also overreacts to that information. Sometimes it forgets things when some other exciting news pops up. The takeaway is this: don't assume that you have access to some unique market moving information that will make you a fortune. Though the efficient markets hypothesis must be taken with a grain of salt, you still must recognize that participants generally have access to much of the same information as you do.

Fundamental Analysis

Reading through the latest USDA report? Pouring through export sales data to get a sense of foreign demand? Evaluating production data for your county? You're performing fundamental analysis. Looking at the fundamentals makes intuitive sense to most of us since the notion of supply and demand isn't that complicated. More supply equals lower price, more demand equals higher price all else being equal.

In my trading days I used to receive a wire from a very seasoned broker who condensed the concept of supply and demand for grain into a very simple story: Imagine total supply as all available stocks in one huge pile. Supply is relatively easy to measure; we just count the bushels produced and add it to existing stocks. For a given marketing year, that's called **beginning stocks**. Next to the pile is a hole, we'll call demand. Demand is a bit more difficult to measure since we really don't know until the end of the year how much was used. At the top of the known quantity (the pile) is a tiny man with a shovel. As we go through the year and grain is used, the tiny man shovels more and more into the hole (demand). If we have a relatively busy month, say huge unexpected export sales, the tiny man must shovel especially fast. During slow periods he gets a break and may slow his shoveling pace.

The point of the story is, we don't know at any given moment precisely how much of the pile will be left when the year ends. This is why the market responds to the export sales report or USDA Supply and Demand reports. This is why fundamental analysis is important.

This brings up an interesting notion: Market expectations versus reality. At any given time there are unknowns in the marketplace. Huge deals are made with only a small number of people aware that they are taking place. Some of the grizzled veterans will remember what has come to be known as "The Great Grain Robbery."

In the summer of 1972, private U.S exporters quietly sold approximately 440 million bushels of wheat to the Soviet Union. To put that figure in perspective, this quantity was equivalent to approximately 30 percent of average US annual production, or 80 percent of total domestic usage (Luttrell). When the sales were finally announced, surprising the market, prices skyrocketed. The market did not expect anything of the magnitude of the Russian sales. Now, it is seldom that activity of this size surprises the market but the moral is simple: the market may expect one outcome when an entirely different one occurs. With every report, the potential for a different reality is presented to the market. The moral is this: don't become too married to a certain outcome. The market is dynamic and anything is possible.

Traders will say they have 'bias' one way or the other. Very seldom do you see someone who is permanently and overtly bullish or bearish.

Because things change, you should concern yourself more with trends than with onetime numbers. The grain robbery aside, usually markets change shape over time, not all at once. So, while the one day 30 cent profit is much sexier and more fun to talk about, it's picking the long term trend that will really make you the expert in your field.

Where to find fundamental information

There are a variety of sources to go for fundamental data. The most readily available and most widely read come from government sources. The USDA pools massive amounts of data into a variety of reports available to the market. There are also a number of private reporting agencies that may provide different opinions than the USDA as well as more specialized data. I'll go over some of the most important and useful sources of information here. These will provide a good starting point for the beginning fundamental analyst.

Government Reports

WASDE- The *World Agricultural Supply and Demand Estimates* report is the quintessential document for anybody wanting information on grain and oilseed supply and use. The WASDE contains **balance sheets** for each crop type that includes a beginning stocks figure, production, use and ending stocks. Essentially all of the elements of supply and demand condensed into a single table. These numbers are scrutinized and argued over by members of the trade; since the report is issued monthly, all of the figures are subject to adjustment (the little man shoveling faster or slower and the pile growing or shrinking).

Export Sales Reports

Every week, usually on Thursday, export sales reports are released. These reports include export sales data by commodity for the prior week. It includes quantities and destinations. Those intimately involved in evaluating these reports will examine the destinations for each commodity looking for unusual tonnages or buyers that rarely purchase. For most of us, the total sales quantity for each commodity is sufficient information.

GTR- Grain Transportation Report

In my opinion this is one of the most underutilized USDA issued reports out there. This weekly report contains information on transportation costs and volumes including rail, truck, barge and ocean freight. By looking at trends in volume and transportation cost, fundamental analysts can get a sneak peak on basis trends.

Prospective Plantings Report

This report is issued at the end of March and offers insight into planting intentions for a variety of crops. Information is broken down by state and commodity with wheat separated out by class. These numbers have obvious implications for fall production figures and the market will respond inasmuch as the reported figures differ from trade expectations.

Quarterly Stocks Report

Issued quarterly, this report contains current stocks figures for a number of different crops including wheat, corn and soybeans. It is a snapshot for a specific timeframe. Imagine taking a picture four times per year of the size of the pile the little man is shoveling from. This report allows for adjustments to be viewed for the overall supply picture. It includes information for grain stored both on and off farms.

Small Grains Summary

Issued in September, this report contains a summary of the previous year's wheat, oats and barley supply figures as well as areas seeded and harvested for the past three years. There aren't projections included in this report but it is very useful for making historical comparisons from one year to the next.

Cattle on Feed Report

No, this report doesn't specifically illustrate grain use but correlations are pretty intuitive. More cattle corresponds to higher feed demand right? So, higher cattle on feed numbers than anticipated ought to be bullish feed grains like corn, sorghum and barley. It's particularly important to evaluate trends when reading the Cattle on Feed report rather than simply draw opinions on viewing a single month's numbers. In other words, you need to see if the number of cattle is increasing or decreasing over time in order to form an opinion on how their numbers correlate to grain demand.

Ethanol Production Report

This is a barometer of domestic corn demand. Obviously, in recent years the ethanol grind has put a big dent in overall corn supplies. Like the Cattle on Feed report, ethanol production will have a direct correlation with grain demand, in this case corn. Again, the trend needs to be evaluated here. In a decreasing margin environment, ethanol plants will reduce their grind and some may even go idle. As margins improve, plants come back online and demand for corn will subsequently increase.

Tracking fundamentals ought to be the bread and butter of your price trend analysis. I knew an elevator manager who routinely kept a T chart of bullish and bearish fundamentals occurring at any given time period. It was a simple way to organize his thoughts that was easy to understand and communicate. I recommend that you come up with a way to track market fundamentals whether it's a T chart or some other technique. You'll gain insights that weren't there before and have a more informed opinion of the business.

Technical Analysis

"A method of evaluating securities by analyzing statistics generated by market activity, such as past prices and volume. Technical analysts do not attempt to measure a security's intrinsic value, but instead use charts and other tools to identify patterns that can suggest future activity (Investopedia)."

There's differing schools of thought on the validity of technical analysis. One side believes its complete hokum; a waste of time and resources trying to predict the future. The other side recognizes that though the past can't predict the future, there are benefits to analyzing price trends that can't be ignored. Because technical analysis involves so much subjectivity, one analyst may come to conclusions that are completely opposite to another analyst. However, the benefits can't be ignored. The key is practice; the trial and error involved with coming up with strategies that work for you.

Trends

Throughout this book, I've talked about trends in price direction. Essentially, a trend is simply the overall direction of prices over a period of time; higher, lower or sideways. For the technical analyst, trends are usually defined by the high and the low price for a given time period. An uptrend would be a succession of higher highs and higher lows. For example, on a daily chart each successive day would have higher high prices *and* higher low prices than the preceding day. Similarly, a downtrend would be a succession of lower highs and lower lows.

Trend lines are a convenient and easy way to evaluate trends and establish **support** or **resistance** levels that may indicate trend reversals. An uptrend line is drawn by connecting two or more low prices in an upward moving market.

Uptrend: March 2015 Corn- Daily Chart

In the trend line drawn in the above chart, a close below the line could indicate a trend reversal; that is to say, the uptrend could be broken and a new trend pointed downward has started. The problem with trend lines is there subjectivity; one person might draw the line different than another. Thus, one chart analyst may have more success in trading with trend lines than the next. This variability can be addressed by using indicators that are less subjective.

Horizontal Trend Line: March 2015 Soybeans- Daily

Downtrend: March 2015 Oats-Daily

Moving averages are easy to use trend analysis tools that don't require you to draw anything; the lines are drawn for you by averaging previous prices. There are essentially two main types of basic moving averages: simple and exponential. The difference between the two is that the exponential moving average provides greater weight to more recent prices when calculating the trend. Older prices carry relatively less weight in calculating the average.

The moving average you use is really a matter of personal preference but I prefer the exponential as recent prices provide more relevant data in my opinion.

Since the moving average is based on prior prices, in order to draw a moving average you'll need to select a timeframe to use. For daily charts, commonly used timeframes are 10, 20, 50 and 100 day. The longer the timeframe the less variable the moving average will be. Visually, longer term moving averages are "flatter" than shorter term ones. See the difference between a 10 day and 50 day moving average below.

10 and 50 Day Exponential Moving Average: July 2015 Wheat Daily

Like a manually drawn trend line, a close above a moving average in a down trending market, or a close below a moving average in an up trending market could signal a trend reversal.

A famous indicator that utilizes moving averages is the 'Bolinger band.' Bolinger bands plot upper and lower ranges that are generally two standard deviations from a moving average. They are useful because they account for volatility in the market.

As the market becomes more volatile, Bolinger bands will widen out (Investopedia). The chart below utilizes a 20 day moving average.

Bolinger Bands: November 2015 Soybeans- Daily

Bolinger bands are used slightly differently than other moving averages in that they are commonly used to estimate **overbought** and **oversold** price levels. Many analysts believe that as prices approach the upper band the market is considered overbought and due for a downward correction. Similarly, when prices approach the lower band the market would be considered oversold and due for a correction to the upside.

Oscillators

Strictly speaking, an oscillator is a 'mathematically derived measure of a market's momentum (Schwager).' To oscillate means to swing or to vacillate between points. So, at their core, oscillators move around a predefined point or set of points. By evaluating a market's momentum, technicians hope to predict future price direction. A slow in momentum could indicate an impending trend reversal. In this way, an oscillator is used as a sort of price notification system. The most commonly used oscillators are stochastics, moving average convergence divergence (MACD) and the relative strength index (RSI).

The stochastic oscillator 'evaluates a market's momentum by determining the relative position of closing prices within the high-low range of a specified number of days.' In general, a stochastic value at or above 70 indicates an overbought market and a stochastic value at or below 30 indicates an oversold market.

Stochastics: December 2015 Corn-Daily

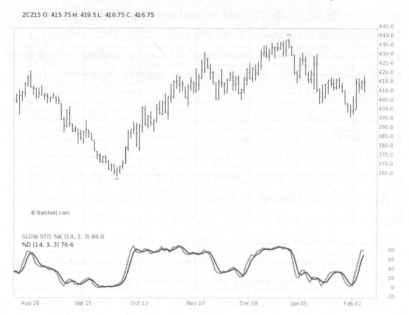

As you can see, the stochastic oscillator is represented by two separate lines: %D and %K. The %K formula is $\%K = 100[(C - L14)/(H14 - L14)]$ where C=the most recent close, L14=the low of the 14 day period and H14=the high of the 14 day period (Schwager). %D is a 3 day moving average of %K. With the stochastic indicator, signals occur when %D crosses through %K. Thomas A. Bierovic advocates the following strategy:

> When stochastic fails to confirm a market's new high, wait for %K to cross below %D and to drop below 70; when stochastic fails to make a new low along with prices, wait for %K to cross above %D and to climb above 30. After identifying a bullish or bearish stochastic divergence, watch the market's price action for a confirming buy or sell signal. (Schwager)

Notice that he recommended waiting for a confirmation. This is common language amongst technicians that basically means, 'don't jump in prematurely.' If you're trading using a daily chart, wait for one more close in the necessary direction before initiating a trade.

The moving average convergence divergence, otherwise known as the MACD is one of my favorite oscillators to use. Like its name suggests, the MACD uses moving averages; so, it's not only an oscillator but also a trend following indicator. The MACD uses the difference between two exponential moving averages (26 day and 12 day). The line generated by this calculation is then plotted over the 9 day exponential moving average. The two, oscillate around each other and their resulting crosses one over the other is a buy or sell indicator.

The chart below illustrates the MACD along with the commonly used MACD histogram. The histogram is the result of subtracting the signal line from the MACD line.

MACD: August 2015 Soybeans-Daily

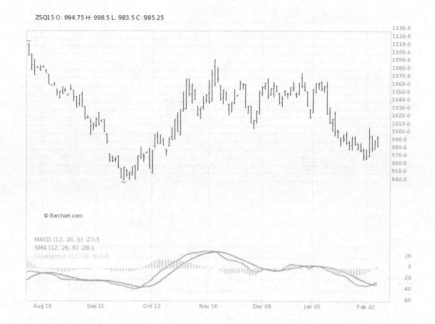

ZSQ15 O: 994.75 H: 998.5 L: 983.5 C: 985.25

MACD (12, 26, 9) -23-5
SMA (12, 26, 9) -28-1
Divergence (12, 26, 9) 4-4

© Barchart.com

The final oscillator I'll cover is the relative strength index or RSI. The RIS is 'a technical momentum indicator that compares the magnitude of recent gains to recent losses in an attempt to determine overbought and oversold conditions of an asset (Investopedia).' Unlike some of the other mathematical indicators, the RSI has a relatively simple formula:

RSI $= 100 - 100/(1 + RS^*)$

*Where RS = Average of x days' up closes / Average of x days' down closes. (Investopedia)

RSI: September 2015 Minneapolis Wheat-Daily

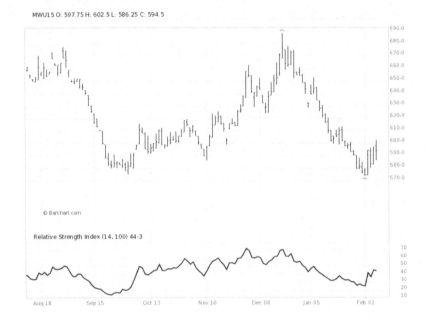

With the RSI, the goal of the technician is once again to estimate levels at which trend reversals take place. Typically, an RSI number above 70 is regarded as overbought and an RSI below 30 is regarded as oversold. Again, it is recommended that you wait for confirmation before initiating a trade based on RSI.

In my opinion, oscillators are an incredibly useful tool in evaluating grain price direction. However, I would strongly recommend that you don't trade solely on oscillator signals. They should be used in conjunction with other technical analysis tools and traders shouldn't jump the gun when initiating trades.

Chart Patterns

Of all the tools available to the technician, chart patterns are possibly the most subjective. Unlike oscillators which are generated using mathematical formulas and frequently have definitive numbers indicating possible reversals, chart patterns are always interpreted in the eye of the chartist herself. So, one chartist may see a reversal where another does not. Evaluating chart patterns is truly why technical analysis is called an art, not a science.

Gaps

A price gap occurs when an entire period's price action is either above (gap higher) or below (gap lower) the previous days price action. In other words, there is an empty space between two consecutive price levels or, a 'gap' in price levels. As a general rule, markets don't like gaps; at some point in the future the market will 'fill' the gap by trading through the gaps range. So, technicians closely monitor them and use them as support or resistance in the future.

Gaps: November 2015 Canola-Daily

Flags and pennants

Flags and pennants are short term consolidation patterns within charts that typically represent pauses in a longer term trend (Schwager). They both represent trading ranges, the difference being greater consolidation is illustrated in a pennant. Flags are pictured with parallel lines while pennants cross.

Signals occur when prices penetrate and close above or below the range of the pennant or flag.

Flags: March 2015 Corn-Daily

Pennant: December 2015 KC Wheat-Daily

Head and Shoulders

The head and shoulders pattern is widely known because it can be a relatively recognizable pattern. It is visible as a three part formation: the middle point (the head) is the highest point with lower points (the shoulders) on each chronological side.

The head and shoulders are not complete until the neckline has been penetrated either to the upside (head and shoulders bottom) or downside (head and shoulders top) (Schwager).

Head & Shoulders: March 2015 Soybean Meal-Daily

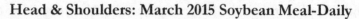

In the chart above, the trend line marks the top of the shoulders also known as the 'neckline' of the pattern. The arrow points to the head. In this chart, the head and shoulders pattern is in fact, incomplete as the neckline hasn't been penetrated to the upside. Rather, prices retreated later in the year.

In psychology, there is a concept known as 'mirroring' that is quite meaningful for traders. Basically, mirroring involves imitation but it goes even further than that. For example, have you ever purchased a new car and then suddenly you notice the same make and model everywhere? Mirroring is a way of subconsciously justifying our actions and preferences.

For the merchant of grain, this means that we have a tendency to see justifications for our existing positions. In other words, as most producers typically hold long positions they have the tendency to have bullish opinions even in falling markets. The latest export sale to Japan, no matter how immaterial it may be is more significant to the bull than record production forecasts and relative lack of demand.

The point I am trying to make is to always be conscious of what the market is telling you. You cannot change price trends simply through the force of your will. Also remember that things change; don't allow yourself to get married to a position and lose money. Allow your opinion to change as the market evolves.

9 PUTTING IT ALL TOGETHER: DEVELOPING YOUR MARKETING PLAN

One of my first Agribusiness courses in college was "Farm and Ranch Management." The Professor was an old Ag Economist who had been involved in agriculture in varied capacities for his entire life. I remember him mentioning his father in law's marketing strategy. He would sell 1/3 of his crop at harvest, 1/3 in December and the other 1/3 he allowed himself to speculate on. At the time I didn't think much of this strategy. As I progressed in the grain industry though, I came to the conclusion that this guy was on to something. If nothing else, at least he had a plan in place! If he did the same thing year in and year out, over time the good and the bad *should* balance each other out. I think it was a bit oversimplified, but at least he had something in place in terms of a strategy.

Far too frequently, farmers don't treat their farming enterprise like a for profit business. Rather, they are content to throw darts when it comes to grain marketing, taking unnecessary risks and limiting their profit potential. Running a successful farming enterprise can be a confusing endeavor that requires you be an expert in so many areas that is tough to keep track. The goal of this chapter is to layout, step by step what it takes to develop a successful grain marketing plan.

In my view, the basics of a successful marketing plan can be condensed into seven steps.

1) Determine your production cost per acre
2) Estimate production, or simply use your proven yields
3) Purchase appropriate levels of crop insurance
4) Determine your breakeven price per bushel
5) Set a target price goal
6) Place open sell orders
7) Re-evaluate as the market changes.

The table below can help organize some of the key figures in the marketing plan into a manageable summary.

Figure 1- Marketing Plan Basics

Key Marketing Figures

Crop Year:	_____		
Commodity:	_____		
Total Production:	_____		
Loan Rate:	_____		
Break Even Price:	_____		
Target Price:	_____		
Historical Basis	Low:	High:	
Sales:	Date:	Quantity:	Price:

Remember, the goal here is to simplify and strategize. If your marketing strategy up to this point has been to throw darts at seemingly attractive prices, this will take some serious effort. However, the peace of mind that comes with having a strategy in place that will actually direct you when to sell is priceless.

How Much New Crop Should I Sell?

One of the most common questions I get when working with producers is 'how much new crop grain do I forward contract?' Fortunately, there is useful information to guide you in making this decision. Your crop insurance coverage makes a big difference in making new crop marketing decisions.

Now, there are some producers who would feel comfortable forward contracting the entire production guarantee that crop insurance offers. Since many of us aren't that risk tolerant I have a calculation that can help. Let's begin with an absolute worst case scenario. If your entire crop is destroyed, what quantity of forward contracted bushels would allow you to breakeven?

Example 1

Let's say you purchased yield protection on your soybean crop at the 85% coverage level. You grow 1,000 acres of soybeans and your APH is 40 bushels per acre. The RMA published a projected price for soybeans at $9.00 per bushel. Furthermore, the current market price for new crop beans is $10.00 per bushel and your production cost is $280 per acre. Let's summarize this information in a more organized way:

APH: 40,000 bushels (40bpa * 1,000 acres)
Insured portion: 34,000 bushels (.85 * 40,000)
Minimum price for insured portion: $9.00/bushel
Current Market price: $10.00/bushel
Production cost: $280/acre
Total production = 0 bushels

There's a convenient formula that can help estimate how much to sell:

(Minimum revenue – Breakeven cost)/(Buyback Price-Indemnity Price)= Quantity available to sell

Your minimum revenue is your insured production * the insured price. In our example it would be 34,000*9.00=$306,000.

Breakeven cost is simply your total cost of production. Ours would be $280*1,000=$280,000. Lastly, the buyback price is the price of soybeans when you contact the elevator and tell them you can't deliver. They will cancel the contract at the market price plus any applicable fee. You'll have to guess on this figure. Let's use a big number so we can plan for the worst. We'll call it $15.00/bushel. Another note: the buyback price-indemnity price must be greater than $1.00 difference. If it's not, don't bother including it in your calculation.

So, plugging these figures into our formula we get:

($306,000-$280,000) = $26,000: Essentially, this number is what you could lose and still break even for the year.

$26,000/ ($15.00-$9.00) =4,333 bushels available to forward contract.

So, if you work under the assumption that you may produce nothing, you could only forward contract 4,333 bushels. The fact however, is that is a very unlikely scenario. (Note, if the insurance price guarantee is greater than the forward market price, always assume zero bushel production in making this calculation.) This is where risk tolerance comes into play. What minimum production would you be comfortable using in making marketing decisions? Let's use 20 bushels per acre.

APH: 40,000 bushels (40bpa * 1,000 acres)
Insured portion: 34,000 bushels (.85 * 40,000)
Minimum price for insured portion: $9.00/bushel
Current Market price: $10.00/bushel
Production cost: $280/acre
Total production = 20,000 bushels

In this example we will receive an indemnity payment on 14 bushels per acre (34-20). So, our minimum total revenue will be:

($9*14*1,000)+ ($10*20*1,000) = $326,000

If we plug these figures into our original formula, it looks like this:

(($326,000-$280,000)/ ($15.00-$9.00))+ 20,000 = 27,666 bushels available to forward contract.

In writing, the final formula looks like this:

((Revenue – Breakeven cost)/ (Buyback Price-Indemnity Price)) + Minimum production= Quantity available to sell

So, under our assumptions we could safely forward contract 27,666 bushels, or 69% of our proven yield. A producer with a higher risk tolerance could go even higher; there's no hard and fast rule. This calculation gives you a baseline to work with. Bear in mind, because prices are fluid there will be some 'play' in these figures. As prices change, your breakeven sales quantity will also change. Since this method is used to give you an estimate on how much to sell, you don't need to re-calculate every day.

Frankly, when you ask your local grain buyer his opinion he'll probably give you some arbitrary number based on his personal preferences. You could ask 10 different merchants and get 10 different answers. This method will give you something to work with that is unique to your operation. Feel free to tweak the numbers to suit your needs.

What shipment period do I sell?

Remember, if the market pays you to store grain (carry), then you store it. If it pays you to sell it now, then sell it now. It's really a simple strategy that can make you money. But, how do you know when the market is paying enough of a carry to justify storing grain? There's an easy formula for that.

Cost of carry = (Forward Price * Interest rate * Days of carry)/360

This formula estimates your cost to store grain on your farm. Let's break it down:

Forward Price: this is a realistic price that you could sell grain at for some future shipment period. For example, if it's January now and you're considering selling corn for June shipment, what price could you realistically sell? Let's assume we can sell $3.50 per bushel.

Interest Rate: This is either the rate of interest you're paying on borrowed funds or the rate you could be getting to invest your money elsewhere. We'll use a rate of 8%

Days of Carry: For that June corn we mentioned earlier, we'd have to store grain for approximately 5 months. Let's call it 150 days.

Cost of carry = ($3.50 * .08 * 150)/360 = 11.6 cents

Over the course of 5 months, that comes to approximately 2.3 cents per month. So, if you can obtain a carry of greater than 2.3 cents per month, it pays to store the grain.

Of course, there are other marginal costs when it comes to storing grain including the cost of the steel itself, fumigation and aeration. I recommend adding an additional ½ to 1 cent per bushel to estimate your costs of carry. Furthermore, if you are storing grain at a commercial grain elevator they are probably charging you a monthly rate. You'll need to add your interest expense to the flat rate in order to come up with a total cost of carry.

Sample Marketing Plans

Everything I've talked about up to this point is designed to help you construct a plan with one goal in mind: to make money. So, let's start building some marketing plans. We'll start very simply; flat price sales only, nothing fancy to confuse the plan.

Figure 2- Sample Marketing Plan #1

<u>Treasure Farm Marketing Plan</u>
Crop: Hard Red Winter Wheat
Total Area Seeded = 1,000 acres
Production cost = $250.00/acre
APH= 45 bushels/acre or 45,000 bushels total production
Crop Insurance = I have elected yield protection at the 85% coverage level.
Break Even Level = $5.55/bushel based on APH yields
Target Price/bushel = $6.50
Forward Contract up to 75% or 33,750 bushels

Pre-harvest Marketing Strategy
Place the following sell orders:
20,000 bushels at $6.50
5,000 bushels at $6.60
5,000 bushels at $6.70
3,750 bushels at $6.80

Place a stop order at $6.00 for whatever hasn't filled, adjusting the quantity each time a sell order fills.

Post harvest Marketing Strategy:
Total Production = 40,000 bushels
Goal: Hold no un-priced wheat beyond May 30th
Place sell order for the balance of crop

Like I said, this strategy is pretty basic but it contains all the necessary information on paper. The point is, you know exactly what you're supposed to do. I've got crop insurance purchased, I know exactly how much I can forward contract before harvest, and I've got sell orders in place. Notice the use of a stop loss order at $6.00 in my pre harvest strategy. If the market is trending lower, I'd still like to realize a profit. Since my breakeven price is $5.55/bushel I can still realize a good profit. Still, I cannot sell more than 75% of my projected production.

Figure 3- Sample Marketing Plan #2

M&S Farm Marketing Plan
Crop: Yellow Corn
Total Area Seeded = 5,000 acres
Production cost = $700.00/acre
APH= 200 bushels/acre or 1,000,000 bushels total production
Crop Insurance = I have elected yield protection at the 75% coverage level.
Break Even Level = $3.50/bushel based on APH yields
Target Price/bushel = $4.50
Forward Contract up to 50% or 500,000 bushels

Pre-harvest Marketing Strategy

Sell 100,000 bushels of Dec $4.50 calls at $0.25 premium

Sell 100,000 bushels basis fixed at -.25CZ

Place the following sell orders:

100,000 bushels at $4.40

100,000 bushels at $4.50

100,000 bushels at $4.60

Place sell stop order for 100,000 bushels at $4.25. If it fills, lift options position.

Post harvest Marketing Strategy

Total production = 900,000 bushels

Goal: Hold no un-priced corn beyond July 31st

Price objective: $4.10

Sell 100,000 bushels and lift options position.

Place the following sell orders:

100,000 bushels at $3.80

100,000 bushels at $4.00

100,000 bushels at $4.20

100,000 bushels at $4.40

Place a sell stop order at $3.75 for anything that hasn't been sold.

This marketing plan incorporated an options strategy in order to improve my net margins. I get to keep the 25 cent premium no matter what happens. If prices rise to $15.00, the options will get exercised but I'll also enter into a cash contract which will offset the loss. Next, we'll incorporate carry's into the equation.

Sean's Farm Marketing Plan

Crop: Yellow Soybeans

Total Area Seeded = 2,000 acres
Production cost = $400.00/acre
APH= 50 bushels/acre or 100,000 bushels total production
Crop Insurance = I have elected yield protection at the 75% coverage level.
Break Even Level = $8.00/bushel based on APH yields
Target Price/bushel = $9.00
Forward Contract up to 60% or 60,000 bushels
Cost to Carry = 6 cents/month
Oct→Dec = 20 cent price carry in the market

Pre-harvest Marketing Strategy
Buy 40,000 bushels of Dec 9.40 puts at .40 cent premium in order to lock in a minimum price.
Place the following sell orders for December:
15,000 bushels at $9.25
15,000 bushels at $9.50
15,000 bushels at $9.75
15,000 bushels at $10.00
Place sell stop order for on any unfilled pre-harvest sales $8.50. Adjust quantity as sell orders fill.

Post harvest Marketing Strategy
Total production = 110,000 bushels
Goal: Hold no un-priced soybeans beyond June 30th
Price objective: $12.00
Place the following sell orders:
Since I own 40,000 bushels of puts giving me a minimum price of $9.00, I'm going to market the rest of my crop more aggressively.
15,000 bushels at $11.50

> 15,000 bushels at $12.00
> 20,000 bushels at $12.50
> If prices retreat, I'll exercise my 40,000 bushel put option and receive $9.00/bushel.

There are a number of different directions you can take with your marketing plan. You've got flexibility to adjust it as the market changes and you realize what your actual production figures will be.

Contract's Available at Your Local Elevator

You don't necessarily have to have a brokerage account to have varied options in marketing your grain. Your local elevator will most likely have an assortment of marketing choices that will allow you to lock in prices when you are ready.

It goes without saying that you need to read and understand the terms of any contract before you sign it. Because terms and conditions vary from one company to another and can even vary between different locations of the same company, doing business with multiple elevators can be confusing. Obtain a copy of the appropriate discount schedules from each elevator and ask frequently if they've made any changes. This way, you can have a good idea of the amount of your check when the company settles up on your grain.

Additionally, always know who you're doing business with. Counter party risk is a very real concern when you're dealing in sizeable dollar amounts. It's not unheard of to see producers hung out to dry on payments for grain that they've shipped when a company goes bankrupt. Don't let that happen to you. Only do business with reputable organizations that you know. If possible, get copies of their financial statements. Incidentally, this is one of the advantages of working with farmer owned Cooperatives. You always have the ability to know whether the company is solvent or not.

With that said, let's continue the discussion with a general overview of contracts available at most grain elevators.

The Delayed Pricing Contract

Sometimes known as the "No Price Established" contract, this is used when you are bullish prices but want to haul grain to the elevator for any reason. Obviously, if you're bearish and you want to haul grain in you'll simply write a cash contract with the elevator.

Elevators will enter into a delayed pricing contract (DP for short) in order to get obtain title to grain that is stored in their facility. The elevator must have title to the grain in order to ship it so in many regions elevator managers will require producers to transfer title. Some areas, where storage space is ample (the PNW for example) allow producers to retain title to hauled grain. For a farmer, this is obviously preferable but either way you'll likely be paying storage charges on anything you've brought to town. Depending on the storage rate and the current market conditions, you may want to write a cash contract anyway.

The Flat Price Contract

The flat price contract is the most commonly used contracting method for grain and oilseed farmers. Though any other contracting method can initiate a trade, in the end every cash sale you make will become a flat price contract. For example, a basis fixed contract will become a flat price contract once the futures portion has been priced. Flat price contracts can be either "spot" (today's price) or forward contracts.

To "flat" a contract simply means to price both the basis and futures components. There is nothing left to do to complete the contract; the trade is completely priced (in contrast to the basis or futures fixed contracts discussed later). This simple fact is really the biggest appeal of this type of contracting method. They're easy to manage and don't require further monitoring. Once it's done, you can move on to your next target price and sale.

In addition to being simple, flat price contracts transfer all downside price risk from the seller to the buyer. Conversely, the seller will lose any opportunity to take advantage of price appreciation on the contracted bushels.

The Basis Fixed Contract

A contracting tool that your local grain elevator should offer is the basis fixed contract. This contract allows you to lock in just the basis portion of a contract price and leave the futures un-priced.

Let's say you forward contract 5,000 bushels of corn for October delivery at your local elevator at a basis of -.40 CZ. Today, futures are at $4.00. In six months you decide to price out the contract. The following table illustrates contract prices under various scenarios.

Table 1- Sample Basis Fixed Contract Outcomes

Futures Price	Basis	Contract Price
$3.00	($0.40)	$2.60
$4.00	($0.40)	$3.60
$5.00	($0.40)	$4.60

Your only remaining price risk is in the futures market. All basis risk has been removed since you already locked in that portion of the contract. But, since you don't have any risk, you also lose the potential reward if basis levels rise.

This type of contract would be used during times when your personal bias is for futures to trend higher over time. Remember, as a general rule, basis is inversely related to futures. If you are on the right side of the market, futures will rise and basis will fall. Obviously, this type of contract isn't without risk. Futures could drop and basis could rise, in which case you are on the wrong side of everything.

The Futures Fixed Contract

The futures fixed contract, sometimes referred to as a "hedge to arrive" or HTA allows you to lock in a futures price and leave the basis pricing open until a later time. HTA's are a commonly used contracting tool that fell out of favor to some extent after the unprecedented rallies of 2008. Still, aside from a flat price cash contract, the HTA is probably the second most frequently used pricing option by farmers.

In general, this type of contract would be used when you are bearish futures and/or bullish basis levels. It allows the seller to remove the futures price risk while simultaneously giving the ability to take advantage of basis rallies; or drops.

Let's say you write a HTA contract with your local elevator for 5,000 bushels of soybeans for October delivery. Presently, November soybean futures are at $12.00 and basis is -.50 SX. Since futures risk is off the table, you're only price risk is in the basis as illustrated in the following table:

Table 2- Sample Futures Fixed Contract Outcomes

Futures Price	Basis	Contract Price
$12.00	$0.00	$12.00
$12.00	($0.50)	$11.50
$12.00	($1.00)	$11.00

The Minimum Price Contract

In Chapter 8 we discussed options as a way to manage risk and improve margins. The minimum price contract is a risk management tool that utilizes call options to create a price floor, which the contracted grain cannot drop below.

This example assumes that you entered into a minimum price contract at $5.90/bushel. The elevator purchased on your behalf, a $6.50 call option at a premium of 40 cents. So, if the futures price drops, you have no risk of depreciation on your cash sale. However, if futures prices rise, you can still take advantage of the rally. Essentially, for the cost of the option you have taken the downside risk off the table.

Table 3- Sample Minimum Price Contract Outcomes

(Basis = -.20)

Current Dec Futures	Current Cash Price	Minimum Price Contract
$6.00	$5.80	**$5.90**
$6.10	$5.90	**$5.90**
$6.20	$6.00	**$5.90**
$6.30	$6.10	**$5.90**
$6.40	$6.20	**$5.90**
$6.50	$6.30	**$5.90**
$6.60	$6.40	$6.00
$6.70	$6.50	$6.10
$6.80	$6.60	$6.20
$6.90	$6.70	$6.30
$7.00	$6.80	$6.40

A variation of this would be a minimum price futures fixed contract. The mechanics are basically the same accept no basis would be priced in. In other words, the basis portion of the flat price would still retain downside risk as well as the opportunity for price appreciation.

Regardless of how you decide to contract grain, the takeaway from this chapter is the importance of creating an outline to help you reach your profit goals. Opening your own brokerage account is very useful, particularly when it comes to hedging your positions and developing more sophisticated marketing strategies. However, even without one your local elevator should have the ability to provide you with a number of marketing tools.

10 SEAN'S RULES FOR GRAIN MARKETING

Over the course of my grain merchandising career, particularly early on, I made plenty of arbitrary and emotional decisions. Some of them turned out to be winners, some turned out to be losers. Throughout this book, I've talked a lot about having a plan in place to avoid making those types of choices in your grain marketing efforts.

As I progressed in my career, I developed a number of rules that helped guide my decision making. I subsequently saw greater success as I gained experience and implemented each rule. Some of my rules have been amended to accommodate a farm business rather than the elevator's that I worked for. Of course, nobody bats 1.000 but my batting average did improve as I became more disciplined.

Rule #1: Don't focus on Prices- Focus on Business Profit

This is my number one rule for very good reason. Too often, I've seen producers become fixated on some arbitrarily high price despite having the opportunity to sell their grain at a profit. So every time you think about selling grain remember, you're in this business for the long haul, always think in terms of profits.

Rule #2: Know your costs of production

It goes without saying that in order to follow rule number one, you have to know where your breakeven price is. Chapter three illustrates a simple method to estimate production costs before planting and calculating exact costs after harvest. By having these figures in hand, you can market your grain year round, forward contracting prior to planting if the market signals indicate a selling opportunity. Don't do business blindly; know your production costs.

Rule #3: When the market inverts, sell the inverse

Speaking of selling opportunities, rules 3 and 4 are here to guide you in listening to the market. An inverse (also known as backwardation), is when the nearby price is higher than deferred prices. Let's say for example that it's March and you have 50,000 bushels of corn stored on your farm and you're opportunistically waiting for the right time to sell. You call your local elevator and get the following flat price bids:

March: $6.00
April: $5.50
May: $5.50

What do you do? Generally, inverses occur either when supplies are low, often times in years when production is down or when there is an artificial kink in the supply chain. This kink could be the result of very little movement at the farm level, transportation disruptions or any number of other possibilities. What's important is what the market is trying to tell you. Inverted markets are signals for producers to sell the nearby shipment period immediately. So, the correct answer to my question is, sell as much as you can execute for March delivery.

There is no reason to carry a depreciating asset which is exactly what is occurring during in an inverted market. You wouldn't hold a stock if you could see into the future and the value was dropping each month would you? Do what the market instructs and sell the nearby.

Rule #4: If the market pays you to carry grain, then carry it

If your cost of storing grain (including interest and the opportunity cost of investing money elsewhere), is less than the carry (sometimes called contango), the market is telling you to store grain and sell deferred shipments. Essentially, the market is attempting to ration the available supply of grain throughout the marketing year. Let's suppose again, that it's March and you've got the same 50,000 bushels of corn stored on your farm. Your local elevator gives you the following flat price bids:

March: $5.50
April: $5.60
May: $5.70

Alright, what do you do this time? Not so fast, we're missing some critical information. Though it looks like you could pocket an extra 10 cents/month, the reality is not quite as spectacular. You need to do a bit of math. Don't forget to include the cost of carrying grain. This includes interest, grain conditioning (fumigant, aeration, etc) and opportunity costs. Let's say your total storage cost is 5 cents per bushel per month. Now, what do you do? Well, it's still profitable to carry. You would sell the carry and earn yourself an additional 10 cents per bushel.

Now, this doesn't necessarily mean you can't to wait to sell, though that may be the correct decision. Read the chapter on forecasting grain prices for more information. At the very least this carry means that if you market your grain today, you should forward contract instead of initiating a spot sale.

Rule #5: Don't allow cash flow needs to dictate when you sell

This is one area where I am bound to have disagreements with producers and other grain marketing experts. I've read plenty of recommendations that suggest timing your sales so that your income arrives at the same time that bills are due. I disagree with this strategy for one major reason: it doesn't facilitate "listening to the market" as rules 3 and 4 mandate and therefore it is not a good strategy for taking advantage of opportunities that are made available to the astute marketer.

Interestingly, since many farmers follow the traditional method of selling for cash flow, prices will become regionally depressed during certain times of the year. For example, in a given area, fertilizer expenses will come due for most farmers at the same time. What do you do? Sell a little grain to cover the expense. The market responds with lower basis levels during that time frame.

In Montana, the months of December and March were typically very busy. It wasn't because prices were always better during these periods; it was because producers wanted money. What does the market do? It drops the basis in order to ration supply. Subsequently, the market frequently creates better selling opportunities in January or April.

Don't get me wrong, selling a little grain once in a while to cover an expense is not a cardinal sin. Invariably you will have times that require you to match up some income with expenses. If however, your entire marketing strategy is based around this method, you're most certainly leaving money on the table. Give yourself marketing flexibility; don't let cash flow dictate your decisions.

Rule #6: Look at the big picture

There is a huge amount of information available to the general public regarding grain markets. International grain tenders are routinely publically available. National and global supply statistics and production information are readily available to anybody who has an internet connection (hopefully that includes all of my readers). The point of staying on top of macro market conditions is to better ascertain market direction as well as give insight into possible sales opportunities.

Production issues in Matto Grasso, Brazil could have big implications for soybean prices. Heavy rainfall in Australia might be bearish for world wheat prices. The key in monitoring market fundamentals is to not allow you to become tricked into a bullish outlook. The Brazilian drought might be offset by record US production. The market tends to price in fundamentals so don't get married to a losing opinion.

More importantly in my opinion, is to monitor international grain tenders that are made public. It's as easy as going to Google and searching for "wheat tenders" or "corn tenders." If the Egyptians buy SRW from the US for February shipment, you may see better selling opportunities for shipment in late January or early February. It's not as clear cut as rules 3 and 4 because here you're in the business of **forecasting** prices, so it's important to continue to listen to the signals the market is sending. The goal is to find clues that might provide insight on price direction.

Rule #7: Buy crop insurance

Crop insurance is a critical component to an effective marketing plan and not just because it protects against disaster. Having insurance coverage on your inventory gives marketing flexibility that you wouldn't otherwise have. Imagine forward contracting new crop soybeans without protection, having no idea whether your production will be sufficient to cover what you sell. In fact, prior to the implementation of federally subsidized crop insurance producers were extremely reluctant to forward contract grain for harvest. Insurance gives you some degree of peace of mind, allowing flexibility in marketing decisions.

Additionally, lenders will generally require minimum levels of crop insurance coverage in order to protect themselves from loss. Since most farms at the very least need additional credit lines in order to manage cash flow needs, you'll need to check with your lender in order to find out their minimum insurance requirements. Then, buy extra.

All the fancy marketing schemes in the world are worthless when a drought destroys your yields and wipes out your overall production. Crop insurance is a key to any comprehensive grain marketing strategy. Don't roll the dice and hope for a big crop. Buy insurance, it's a rule.

Rule #8: Go for singles, not home runs

See rule number 1. Hey, speculating on a small part of your overall production is perfectly acceptable as long as you've properly budgeted for any negative contingencies. Left unchecked, the lust for that one big trade can result in some major lost opportunities. In 2008, one of the manager's of my company's grain elevators bid a local producer $21/bushel for 100,000 bushels of his spring wheat. He wanted to hold out for $30. Eventually he sold it for something close to $11/bushel. Not a bad number in the whole scheme of things but $1,000,000 less than he could have netted. This rule suggests treating your farm like a business; not a speculative trading house.

Swinging for the fences on every sale is not a sustainable way of doing business. Farming is risky enough without striking out on grain sales. Make profitable sales, don't take unnecessary risks.

Rule #9: Stick to your marketing plan

This pretty much sums things up. Your marketing plan takes the guesswork out of marketing decisions. Stick to it and you'll have an easier time sleeping at night and a better chance of staying in business year in and year out.

Your marketing plan should guide your decision making. Because you know exactly what it takes to make a profit; you know exactly what it costs to store grain on your farm; you know when to sell. As a result, you don't leave yourself room for emotional decisions.

Grain marketing doesn't have to be bewildering. In this short book, I've summarized basic ideas and techniques that are designed to simplify the process. The key for the grain marketer is to plan. Plan your marketing strategies. Plan on building a profitable, long term business that you can share with your family. It is my hope that you will be in business for years to come. May you long feed the world, one bushel at a time.

Bibliography

AP. "Ore. Dust Storm Causes Fatal Pileup." 25th September 1999.
    http://www.apnewsarchive.com/1999/Ore-Dust-Storm-
    Causes-Fatal-Pileup/id-
    90d487ad96d65c6c1b37149fc8bba369. Electronic. 14th
    January 2015.

CFTC. "Disaggregated Commitments of Traders ." 13 January 2015.
    http://www.cftc.gov/dea/futures/ag_lf.htm. 19 January
    2015.

Chabris, Christopher and Daniel Simons.
    http://theinvisiblegorilla.com/blog/2011/04/20/gorillas-
    working-memory-and-the-media/. 20 April 2011. 8 February
    2015.

Edwards, William. "Twelve Steps to Cash Flow Budgeting." April
    2014.
    http://www.extension.iastate.edu/agdm/wholefarm/html/c
    3-15.html. 18 January 2015.

Investopedia.
    http://www.investopedia.com/terms/b/bollingerbands.asp.
    n.d. 7 February 2015.

—. *http://www.investopedia.com/terms/r/rsi.asp.* n.d. 7 February
    2015.

—. *http://www.investopedia.com/terms/t/technicalanalysis.asp.*
    n.d. 7 February 2015.

Iowa State University. "Grain Options Boost Marketing Flexibility."
    n.d.

*http://www2.econ.iastate.edu/faculty/wisner/GRAINOPTIO
NSBOOSTMARKETINGFLEXIBILITY02.htm.* 1 July 2014.

Kay, Ronald D and William M. Edwards. *Farm Management- 4th ed.*
Fairfield, PA: Edward E. Bartell, 1999.

Kub, Elaine. *Mastering the Grain Markets: How Profits Are Really
Made.* United States of America: Create Space, 2014.

Luttrell, Clifton B. "The Russian Wheat Deal- Hindsight vs.
Foresight." October 1973.
*https://www.staff.ncl.ac.uk/david.harvey/MKT3008/Russia
nOct1973.pdf.* 5 February 2015.

Morgan, Dan. *Merchants of Grain.* New York: Penguin Books, 1980.

Plastina, Alejandro and William Edwards. "Proven Yields and
Insurance Units for Crop Insurance." September 2014.
*http://www.extension.iastate.edu/agdm/crops/html/a1-
55.html.* 22 January 2015.

Plastina, Alejandro. "Crop insurance policies in 2014." October 2014.
*http://www.agrisk.umn.edu/Library/Display.aspx?RecID=70
98.* 14 January 2015.

—. "Current Crop Insurance Policies." October 2014.
*http://www.extension.iastate.edu/agdm/crops/html/a1-
48.html.* 27 January 2015.

Schwager, Jack D. *Schwager on Futures.* United States of America:
John Wiley & Sons, Inc, 1996.

Stebbins, Christine. "High cash rents to squeeze U.S. Midwest grain
farmers in 2014." *Reuters* 24th December 2013: Web.
Electronic.

USDA AMS. "http://www.ams.usda.gov/mnreports/jo_gr112.txt."
16 June 2014. *www.ams.usda.gov.* 14 November 2014.

USDA. "Grain Transportation Report." 25 September 2014.
*http://www.ams.usda.gov/AMSv1.0/getfile?dDocName=ST
ELPRDC5109110&acct=graintransrpt.* 30th September 2014.

—. "World Agricultural Supply and Demand Estimates." 11
September 2014.
*http://usda.mannlib.cornell.edu/usda/waob/wasde//2010s/
2014/wasde-09-11-2014.pdf.* 26 September 2014.

USDA-RMA. "SUMMARY OF CHANGES FOR THE COMMON CROP
INSURANCE POLICY." April 2010.
http://www.rma.usda.gov/policies/2011/11-br.pdf. 14
January 2015.

Glossary

Actual Production History (APH) - Production history consisting of a minimum of four years and a maximum of ten years. Used to set the guarantees in crop insurance policies.

Aflatoxin- a carcinogen produced by specific molds, which grow on corn and other crops.

At the money- An option with a strike price that is equal to the current market price of the underlying futures contract.

Backwardation- See "inverse"

Baltic Dry Index-The BDI is a number issued by the Baltic Exchange that serves as an indicator for current dry bulk shipping costs in ocean going vessels.

Basis- the difference between the flat price and the futures price at a given delivery point. Basis = Flat Price – Futures Price

Beginning Stocks- All of the grain or oilseed by type and class available in all positions at the beginning of the marketing year. Equivalent to the prior marketing years ending stocks figure.

Call option- The right but not the obligation to buy a specific futures contract at a specific strike price.

Carry- A market in which an assets value is greater in deferred periods than it is in nearby periods.

Clearinghouse-A clearinghouse reduces risks in futures exchanges by netting offsetting transactions across multiple parties. Essentially, when you buy and sell in the futures market you don't need to trade with the same opposing party to offset each trade, the clearinghouse will offset it for you. The existence of a clearinghouse adds liquidity to the market.

Commodity Exchange Price Provisions (CEPP) - CEPP specifies how and when the projected and harvest price components will be determined by crop.

Day order- A futures order that remains open only until the end of the trading day. If it does not fill it is automatically cancelled.

Deferred- A generic term meaning any timeframe beyond the nearby month. Generally traders use this term to characterize shipments more than two months out. For example, if it's currently January, March or April and beyond would be considered a deferred months.

Delta- A metric that measures the movement in an option premium given a specific unit change in the underlying futures price.

Demurrage- A fee charged by shipping companies when product is not loaded or unloaded in a timely manner. Rail, barge and vessel owners will allow a specific amount of time for equipment to sit idle before assessing the charge as an incentive to keep their equipment moving as often as possible, thus ensuring quicker turnover.

Derivative- A contract whose value is derived from an underlying asset. For example, options contracts are derived from futures.

Despatch- A payment from a vessel owner to an export terminal for loading in a timely manner. An economic incentive similar to demurrage, despatch acts as a carrot to load as fast as possible.

Ending Stocks- All of the grain or oilseed by type and class available in all positions at the end of the marketing year.

Exchange- An exchange is a central marketplace where participants can buy and sell a standardized product. All contracts have a very specific set of terms that apply to them.

Exercise- In options, the act of putting into effect the right specified in the options contract. When an option is exercised, the underlying futures are assigned to both buyer and seller as outlined in the options contract.

Expiration- The date at which a futures or options contract ceases trade. Options positions that are not offset expire worthless. Futures are subject to physical delivery.

Fill or kill- A futures limit order that is either filled immediately or cancelled.

Fixed Costs- Production expenses which are unrelated to yields or revenues. For example, in a cash rent agreement, you must pay rent whether you produce a crop or not.

Forecasting- Efforts to predict grain price direction. Methodologies include technical and fundamental analysis.

Gamma- An options metric that measures how fast the delta changes as the underlying futures contract changes.

Good til Cancelled (GTC) - A futures order that remains open until it is filled or cancelled by the account holder.

Grain Transportation Report (GTR)- A weekly report issued by the USDA that includes information on rail, barge, truck and ocean freight trends and prices.

Green snap- A term used to describe the breaking of a corn stalk due to high winds.

Initial Margin- The dollar amounts of traders own funds that must be deposited with a brokerage in order to initiate futures trades.

Inter-Market spread-A spread that involves buying a contract of one product and selling a completely different product. For example, buying Dec Corn and selling Dec wheat.

Intra-Market spread-A calendar spread buying a futures contract of one month and selling a different month of the same commodity.

In the money- An option is characterized as in the money when it has value in being exercised. A call option with a strike price that is below the current market price or a put option with a strike that is higher than the current market price.

Intrinsic Value- The difference between an option strike price and the underlying futures price.

Inverse-A market in which an assets value is greater in the nearby shipment period than it is in deferred shipment periods.

Leverage- the use of borrowed money to enhance returns. Futures transactions are leveraged since they are generally traded on margin.

Limit order- An order to buy or sell futures at a specific price level.

Loss Limit- A figure that represents the percentage of the expected county yield at which no additional indemnity amount is payable. Currently set at 0.18

Maintenance Margin- The minimum amount of funding that a trader must maintain with a brokerage in order to hold a position.

Market if touched (MIT)- The opposite of a stop order. An MIT is placed in the money and converts to a market order when touched.

Market on open (close) - A futures order to buy or sell at the market only during the opening or closing minute of the appropriate market.

Market order- An order to buy or sell futures at the best currently available price.

Option writer- The seller of an option contract.

Out of the money- An option that has no intrinsic value. A call option with a strike price that is higher than the current market or a put option with a strike that is lower than the current market.

Overbought- A term used in technical analysis to indicate that prices have risen to a level that is presently unsustainable and is due for a downward correction.

Oversold- A term used in technical analysis to indicate that prices have fallen to a level that is presently unsustainable and is due for an upward correction.

Paper market- A cash market with standardized delivery points and grade specifications. Commercial traders use paper markets to manage their net positions.

Projected Price- Prices used by the RMA to determine crop insurance guarantee levels. These prices are based on futures closing prices for a specified period for each crop.

Protection Factor- A factor that adjusts the amount of coverage, in ARPI policies. Between 0.8 and 1.2

Put Option- The right but not the obligation to sell a specific futures contract at a specific strike price.

Resistance- A term used in technical analysis used to indicate a price level which the market is not expected to surpass.

Rolling a position-The act of liquidating a position in one delivery period and moving it to another. For example, as first notice day approaches for March Soybeans, you'll need to lift your short position and move it to May. You would roll by buying March and selling an equal quantity for May shipment. This term applies to both cash and futures markets.

Self Insure-A risk management strategy in which the insured retains risk rather than transferring it to a third party. Generally, funds will be set aside to cover any potential losses.

Stop order- Sometimes referred to as a "stop loss" order. An order to buy or sell that is placed out of the money. For example, a sell stop would be placed below the price currently trading. Converts to a market order when the target price is touched.

Stop limit order- Much like a sell stop except instead of converting to a market order, it converts to a limit order when the target price is touched. No guarantee of filling.

Strike Price- The specific price at which an option contract can be exercised. The strike price is fixed at the time an option is traded.

Support- A term used in technical analysis used to indicate a price level which the market is expected to not fall below.

Tender- A formal invitation for offers for a specific class, quality and shipment period. The tender announcement details specific terms and conditions that sellers must abide by if they wish to participate in the process.

Time decay- The tendency for options premiums to decrease as the option approaches expiration.

Time Value- The amount of an options premium that can be attributed to the amount of time remaining before expiration. The longer the life of the option, the higher the time value.

Theta- An options metric that measures the rate at which an options' time value decreases.

Variable Costs- Costs that vary depending on overall production. Fertilizer and fuel are possible examples of variable costs.

Vega- An options metric that measures the overall riskiness of the market.

Index

Made in the USA
Monee, IL
17 November 2023

46831128R00090